INTRODUCTION	6
ESSENTIALS	10
BREAKFAST	16
CHICKEN	38
BEEF	72
FISH	106
SAUCES	124
ROASTED VEGETABLES	144
GUEST FEATURES	154
CLOSING	188
GLOSSARY	190

INTRODUCTION

Some people are born with the ability to sing. Some can dance, some can draw. Well, I can't do any of those things, but I can cook.

The entirety of my creative expression comes out through my food. For as long as I can remember, I have always been drawn to the kitchen. When I was very young I visited my uncle, Chris Johnson, in New York City. At the time he owned a restaurant in the East Village that would change my life forever.

One night he brought me to the kitchen where my gaze was met by a strikingly large and fully cooked red snapper. Its bulging eyes were staring right at me as it gave off the most incredible smell my nose had ever sniffed. I was shocked, amazed, and hungry all at the same time. From that point on, cooking became a main staple in my life.

I worked in restaurant kitchens throughout high school. In college, I started my own catering company, which eventually turned into a partnership with one of the top bars on campus where I wrote and ran a late-night food and brunch menu. I ended up dropping out and traveling through Asia, cooking in kitchens, and eating everywhere I went. From this, I gained a whole new understanding of flavor and amassed a new arsenal of useful skills and techniques in the kitchen—which helped me immensely when competing on the Food Network show *Chopped*, where I had the honor of cooking for Martha Stewart. I hope to pass all those skills along to you through this book.

Traditional cookbooks are weighed down with fancy terms and difficult instructions. Most of the time you'll read a recipe that is way too complex and quit before even getting started. Those books assume you already know how to cook, they don't teach you the underlying techniques and methods needed to cook. It's time for a cookbook that bypasses all the bullshit. Something easy; something that anyone can pick up and use regardless of experience level.

Cooking doesn't have to be a daunting task, or something you only think about once a year during Thanksgiving after your fourth beer. This cookbook will provide you with the very basics of how to cook. I assume if you're reading this book, you may not know the difference between a sauté pan and a saucepan—that's totally fine, you're about to learn.

NOT YOUR MOTHER'S COOKBOOK

We will start with simple skills and techniques, and eventually learn to build off of those. You can't be expected to make a beautiful chicken alfredo pasta if you don't first know how to properly cook a chicken breast. You can't learn how to make sauces if you don't first understand what creates thickness in a sauce. You need to start from the bottom and build your way up, dish by dish, ingredient by ingredient.

By the end of this book, I am confident that even the most novice of home cooks will have a general understanding of cooking. You will be able to cook for yourself and others without any of the stress that comes with being in the kitchen.

It should be noted that I didn't invent any of these techniques myself. You can't possibly pinpoint one person as the creator of any basic cooking method—they belong to the universe of cooking as a whole. Cooking is constantly evolving, and there are multiple ways of achieving the same result. I will attempt to teach you the simplest form of each method. From that, I have developed recipes to make full dishes out of the methods you learned. As you begin to build your own skills as a cook, you may find more advanced methods that work for you.

How to use this book

This book is designed to be read chronologically from beginning to end. Each section prepares you for the next as we build in complexity. Taking the time to understand and practice the underlying cooking techniques of each dish will increase your learning curve in the kitchen. Get comfortable with these methods by cooking breakfast and chicken first then moving on to more complex proteins such as beef and fish. If you are going to jump around through this book at the very least you should read the introduction of each section before skipping ahead. If you are new to cooking you might fuck up some recipes here and there—that's part of the experience. Do not get discouraged, and do not quit—nobody gets it right their first time.

I do not recommend following the times in the recipes to the exact minute. Use time in this book more as a general guideline; every stove is different, and every pan conducts heat differently than others—this all plays a factor into the cook time of a dish. I will expand on this later in the book.

I will do my best to explain the cooking terms I am using as I go, but know that if you are ever unsure about what something means there is a glossary in the back of this book with definitions of all the terms I am using. You'll also notice that there are QR codes throughout this book, which when scanned will take you to a short video demonstrating the techniques I am trying to teach. If you are ever confused I highly recommend scanning those and watching the short video. If you would like to see full cooking demonstrations of the more complex recipes in this book, those can be found on my YouTube page by scanning here:

NOT YOUR MOTHER'S COOKBOOK

Salt

Before we get started, let's talk about salt. Arguably the biggest mistake home cooks make is under-salting their food. Salt is crucial when it comes to cooking. It's what will take a dish from average to "holy fuck." Salt enhances flavor, it does not change it. To demonstrate this, take a strawberry and bite into it. Pretty good right? Now take the tiniest bit of salt and put it on the strawberry, let it sit for a minute and then taste it again. If you salted it properly you should not taste any salt but rather the flavor of the strawberry should be more intense. This is what salt does to food when used properly. Another example that you might be familiar with is salted vs. unsalted butter. If you've ever accidentally used unsalted butter on toast you've experienced the offputting taste of something that isn't properly salted. Yet when you use salted butter notice how it doesn't have a salty taste but rather a full-bodied buttery flavor. This is the magic of salt.

Everybody responds to salt differently; some people are more sensitive to salt than others, which causes the perfect salt level to vary from person to person. When a recipe says 'salt to taste', it does not mean salt until your food tastes salty. Your food should never taste salty. What it means is taste your food, then add a bit of salt, then taste again. A huge part of cooking that is often forgotten is tasting as you go. You should constantly be tasting your food as you cook and salting accordingly. Do not wait until the very end of the cooking process to salt a dish, rather taste and salt each time you add a new layer to a dish.

This may sound confusing but when tasting try not to focus on if you can taste salt or not, rather taste for the intensity of an ingredient. Does this tomato sauce taste intense or can it be taken up a notch? This is a skill that takes time to develop, but the more you cook and the more you taste the quicker you will pick it up.

In this book I will often say add a pinch of salt—this equates to ½ a teaspoon. It should be noted as well that I am cooking with Kosher salt (this is what I recommend for you to use as well). Sea salt is great but it is expensive; it can be used as a finishing salt to complete a dish, but it is not necessary when salting throughout the cooking process.

Let's say you've over-salted something. What do you do? You can counteract salt by adding an acidic ingredient to the dish such as vinegar or citrus juice. Sugar can also be effective in counter-balancing salt.

Finally, people often lump salt and pepper together as seasonings. This is not correct; salt is a seasoning, whereas pepper is a spice. Salt enhances flavor, whereas pepper alters it. Pepper does not need to be added every time salt is. Get yourself a pepper mill—you should be freshly cracking pepper every time you cook. You should not be using pre-ground black pepper.

Other seasonings and spices

Building off of salt and pepper, you should always have on hand a good bottle of olive oil and a bottle of vegetable oil for pan frying. For the very basics, this is all that is required. However, as you move on to cooking more advanced recipes you will need more seasonings and spices. You will slowly build your spice cabinet by buying individual spices as required for certain recipes—but it is more cost-effective to buy them all at once as a set.

I always have on-hand some garlic powder, onion powder, paprika, chili powder, cayenne pepper, cumin, chili flakes, allspice, curry powder, and a variety of dried herbs.

You will often see recipes using spices that come from peppers. The most common are paprika, cayenne, chili flakes, and chili powder. Paprika comes from sweet red and orange peppers. It adds a mild sweet pepper flavor to dishes as well as a bright red color. It goes well with chicken, eggs, and root vegetables. Cayenne comes from a variety of spicy chili peppers. If you want to make a dish spicy use cayenne, just know it can be very strong and overpowering so use it in small doses. Chili flakes can also add heat to a dish. They come from drying and crushing whole chilies, seeds and all. Chili powder is a mixture of pepper spices including cayenne and paprika, as well as other spices such as cumin, onion powder, and oregano. It has a flavor you would associate with Tex-Mex cooking.

Spices such as garlic powder, onion powder, mustard powder, ginger powder, as well as any dried herbs provide the flavor you would associate with their fresh counterparts. If you do not have a fresh ingredient it can be substituted with the dried version, just know that when you dry something out it becomes more intense in flavor so you will need less of it than if it were fresh. A general rule of thumb is if a recipe calls for 1 tablespoon of a fresh ingredient you can substitute that for 1 teaspoon of the dried ingredient.

Pantry items

Aside from spices, here are some other pantry items I recommend having. These have a very long shelf life, so once they are purchased they will last for a while.

- All-purpose flour
- Corn starch
- Baking powder
- Bread crumbs
- Sugar (white and brown)
- Vinegars (white wine, balsamic, and apple cider)

Going off of that, here is the equipment I recommend you have in your kitchen:

Equipment

Knives

Knives are an essential part of becoming a good cook. In the same way an artist needs a brush to paint, a chef needs a knife to cook. There are many different knives that are used for various tasks, but for the purposes of this book you can get through every recipe with only a chef's knife. If I were to recommend three knives to purchase they would be a chef's knife, a paring knife (small knife for peeling and paring fruits and vegetables), and a serrated knife (used for slicing bread).

Your chef's knife will become an extension of your hand, so get used to holding it. The proper way to grip a chef's knife is to grasp where the steel meets the handle with your thumb and forefinger.

Keep your knife extremely sharp—a dull knife is more dangerous than a sharp one. A dull knife can easily slip off of the ingredient you are cutting and slice right into your finger. The easiest way to keep your knives sharp is to have them sharpened by a professional. If cared for properly this only needs to be done once or twice a year.

Scan here to watch a more detailed video on knife skills:

NOT YOUR MOTHER'S COOKBOOK

Hand Tools

Metal spatula: Used for flipping when using a stainless steel pan.

Rubber spatula: Used for flipping when using a nonstick pan.

Rubber scraper: Flexible spatula often associated with baking. You will use this when making soft scrambled eggs.

Whisk: Used to combine wet and dry ingredients.

Tongs: Primarily used to flip proteins such as poultry, beef and pork. Fish is too delicate and should be flipped with a spatula.

Slotted spoon: Used for removing foods from oil or a cooking liquid.

Wooden spoon: Used for general stirring.

Multi-purpose box grater: Purchase a cheese grater that has multiple sizes for grating. This way you can use it for grating cheese as well as finely zesting lemons and everything in between.

Mesh strainer and/or sieve: Used for draining pasta and can be used as a filter when making sauces and gravies.

Pots & Pans

You will see the terms sauté pan, frying pan and skillet often when reading recipes. For the purpose of this book those can all be used interchangeably. A frying pan and a skillet are the exact same thing, however, a sauté pan is slightly different. A sauté pan has straight edges where a frying pan/skillet has curved ones.

A sauté pan has slightly more surface area and higher sides, making it slightly more ideal for pan frying and creating pan sauces. That being said, a frying pan will work for everything in this book. Personally, I have one of each and I use them interchangeably, usually I'm grabbing whichever is clean. When I refer to a pan, always assume I mean a stainless steel pan unless specifically stated otherwise.

Nonstick frying pan: Used for lower temperature cooking. This should never be used with metal utensils, only rubber. In this book you will only ever be cooking breakfast dishes in a nonstick pan.

Stainless steel frying pan or sauté pan: The majority of the cooking that you will do will be in this pan. If you can, I recommend spending a little more money on this. When you purchase a higher quality pan, it will conduct heat better making it easier to cook food evenly and regulate temperature. I also recommend getting pans that have steel handles rather than rubber/plastic ones. Metal handles allow you to put the pans in the oven, making them more versatile.

Saucepan: Small pot with a long handle used to make, you guessed it, sauces.

Saucepot and/or stockpot with a lid: This is a pot you would associate with cooking pasta. You will also use it for braising and making stew. A stockpot is just a slightly taller saucepot. For the purposes of this book a saucepot will suffice. Again, try to avoid rubber or plastic handles.

Sheet tray: A rectangular pan with shallow sides used for baking and roasting.

Roasting tray: Similar to a sheet tray but with medium-high sides. For the purposes of this book a sheet tray will suffice. A large sauté pan with a metal handle can become a makeshift roasting tray.

NOT YOUR MOTHER'S COOKBOOK

BREAKFAST

Breakfast is a great place to begin building your cooking skills and playing around with different flavor combinations. In this section, you will learn heat control skills that you'll apply to more advanced cooking later in the book.

The beautiful thing about breakfast is that it's cheap. If you fuck up and flip a pancake too early, you throw away about thirty cents; but fuck up and flip a steak too early—well then, there goes thirty dollars. Frying an egg in hot oil will get you comfortable with heat control. Messing around with different meat/vegetable combinations in omelets will help you develop a sense of flavor profiles, while the process of making light and fluffy scrambled eggs will teach you the importance of good technique and attention to detail.

Breakfast was the first thing I learned how to cook and to this day it is my favorite meal of the three. I remember being a little kid and watching Bobby Flay on the cooking channel early on Saturday morning, and then running into the kitchen to try and recreate what I had just seen. I think the biggest appeal for me at the time was how much sugar and sweetness can be a part of breakfast. The idea of pouring warm maple syrup over a pile of French toast covered with melting butter and powdered sugar was too hard for 10-year-old me to pass up. I don't think there's a better way to start off a lazy weekend morning than with a killer breakfast.

Tip: Scrambled eggs should not be cooked to a point where there are large individual chunks of hard scrambled eggs. Unfortunately, that's the way the majority of people cook their eggs. Hell, that's how my dad cooked them for me when I was growing up—but that's all wrong.

Scrambled eggs should be soft and creamy. They should move together as one unit. You should have small curdles rather than large chunks of cooked egg. You can go crazy low and slow like I'm about to explain, or you can turn the heat higher and cook them faster. Either way, you should be left with light and fluffy eggs.

Once you know how to perfectly scramble eggs, you can apply this method to making a Tex-Mex breakfast stable, the Migas Taco (page 22).

AMERICAN DINER-STYLE EGGS

3 eggs

2 Tbsp of butter

Pinch of salt & pepper

Serves 1

Personally I tend to cook my eggs low and slow as you will learn on the following page. However, if time is of the essence or I am making eggs for a breakfast sandwich this style works very well. You will cook the eggs on a higher heat, creating ripples in the eggs and folding them on top of themselves. This will yield a scrambled egg dish that is soft and fluffy like an omelet and will only take around 1 minute to cook to completion.

1. Beat the eggs together in a bowl until the yolks and whites are evenly combined.

2. Place a nonstick pan on medium heat.

3. Allow the pan to heat up for 3 minutes. For this method, you want a hotter pan.

4. Once the pan is hot, add the butter.

5. When the butter has melted completely and begins to bubble, pour in the eggs, and let them sit in the pan for around 15 seconds. You should see them beginning to change to an opaque color, cooking in an even layer.

6. Using a spatula pull the egg layer from the edges of the pan into the center to create ripples of egg.

7. Continue pulling the egg layer on top of itself until the eggs have set and there is no more liquid egg filling the empty space in the pan.

8. This whole process should take around 1 minute.

9. Finish with a pinch of salt and pepper.

NOT YOUR MOTHER'S COOKBOOK

LOW AND SLOW SCRAMBLED EGGS

3 eggs

2 Tbsp butter

Pinch of salt & pepper

Serves 1

If you've never made eggs over a very low heat, you're in for a huge surprise. Get ready to taste the most flavorful eggs you've ever had, with nothing but eggs, butter, salt, and about 10 minutes of gentle stirring. The key to this method is low heat, constant motion, and plenty of butter.

1. Beat the eggs together in a bowl until the yolks and whites are evenly combined.

2. Place a nonstick pan on low heat.

3. Add the butter and wait for it to melt completely.

4. Once the butter is melted pour in the beaten eggs.

5. Using a rubber scraper, continuously move the eggs; at first it may seem like nothing is happening but the eggs are slowly beginning to cook. Trust me, if you continue to move the eggs for 10–12 minutes you will be blown away by the end result. If the eggs appear to be cooking too fast (i.e. you are getting big curdles), take your pan off the heat for a brief moment and continue to stir. The pan holds enough residual heat to continue cooking the eggs.

6. Once the eggs come together, remove them from the heat and add salt and pepper to taste.

7. You may think the eggs are undercooked because you are used to them being chunky and in individual curdles, don't worry, they are fully cooked. Any more cooking will ruin the masterpiece you have just created.

8. Serve the eggs on freshly toasted bread of your choosing.

20   BREAKFAST

MIGAS TACOS

3 eggs

A handful of corn tortilla chips

⅓ cup of salsa of your choosing

⅓ cup shredded cheese (I use pepper jack)

1 jalapeño, with the seeds removed and finely diced

½ yellow onion, diced

2 Tbsp of butter

Pinch of salt & pepper

5–7 tortillas for serving

Salsa verde & cilantro for garnish

Serves 2

Tip: To warm tortillas, heat them over an open flame or wrap them in tin foil and place them in a 200°F oven for 10 minutes.

1. Beat the eggs together in a bowl until the yolks and whites are evenly combined.

2. Break up a handful of tortilla chips into the beaten eggs and stir.

3. Stir ⅓ cup of salsa into the egg and chip mixture.

4. Dice the onion and jalapeño. (Remove the seeds from the jalapeño by cutting it open lengthwise then scooping out the seeds and the white pith with a spoon.)

5. Place a nonstick pan on medium-high heat and sauté the onion and jalapeño using 1 tablespoon of butter and a pinch of salt and pepper. (To sauté means to cook something quickly at a high heat. Don't be afraid of this word, all you have to do is cook the onions and peppers until they begin to turn brown. The veggies should sizzle when they hit the pan.)

6. Reduce the heat to low and add the remaining tablespoon of butter to the veggies.

7. Pour in the egg mixture and stir continuously until scrambled (the eggs should be soft and fluffy like the soft scrambled method you learned previously, they should not break apart into individual clumps, if that happens you have over scrambled).

8. Add the cheese and remove the pan from the heat.

9. Season the eggs with a pinch of salt and pepper.

10. Stir to combine the cheese with the eggs and veggies, the residual heat in the pan will melt the cheese.

11. Spoon the eggs into warm tortillas.

12. Top the tacos with salsa verde and cilantro.

NOT YOUR MOTHER'S COOKBOOK 23

THE ULTIMATE FRIED EGG

1 egg

3 Tbsp of olive oil, or enough to coat the pan with a quarter-inch of oil

Serves 1

Tip: Unlike the previous methods of cooking eggs, we will not be using a nonstick pan for the crispy egg. The egg will stick to the pan at first; you will be tempted to scrape at it, in turn breaking the egg. You must be patient and wait for the bottom of the egg to go crisp and release from the pan.

This skill of waiting for an ingredient to become unstuck from a pan will be one of the most important ones to master—you'll come to see that you use it when cooking every protein in this book.

This method for frying an egg is all about learning to be comfortable with heat. You're going to be cooking at a high heat. This technique will come in handy when you are searing meats—you must be comfortable with spitting oil, some smoke, and heat blowing in your face. This method yields a beautifully fried egg with crispy edges on the whites and a soft gooey yolk.

1. Crack the egg onto a bowl, do not beat.

2. Place a stainless steel or cast iron pan on medium-high heat.

3. Let the pan sit on the stove and come to temperature for about 3 minutes.

4. Pour in the olive oil. It should coat the pan completely (the oil should be shimmering).

5. Once the pan is hot gently pour in the egg from your bowl.

6. The oil will begin to spit up as the egg whites bubble. This is a good thing, don't bitch out and turn the heat down.

7. Take a spoon and baste the hot oil over the top of the egg if you would like the whites over the yolk to be cooked. (Basting is when you spoon a hot liquid over food to cook it, add flavor, and/or keep it moist when roasting.)

8. The entire cooking process should take around 1 minute and 30 seconds.

9. Remove the egg with a slotted spatula.

10. Salt and pepper to taste.

THE SIMPLE OMELET

3 eggs

⅓ cup of cheese of your choosing

2 Tbsp of butter

Pinch of salt & pepper

Serves 1

Tip: Building off of this technique, you can create all sorts of delicious omelet combinations.

The perfect omelet all comes down to texture. You want it to be light and fluffy—you do not want to scald your eggs. Your omelet should not be brown, but rather a golden yellow with a silky smooth inside. A perfectly cooked omelet will yield a gooey center without even having to add cheese. Much like scrambled eggs, the key to a perfect omelet comes down to heat control and patience.

1. Beat the eggs together in a bowl until the yolks and whites are evenly combined.

2. Place a nonstick pan on medium heat and add the butter.

3. Once the butter is melted pour in the eggs.

4. Let the eggs set for around 30 seconds, then using a rubber spatula, begin to pull the layer of cooked egg from the edges of the pan slightly into the center. The egg should hold to where you pull, creating a ripple of egg.

5. Tilt the pan to move the uncooked layer of egg into the now vacant area in the pan.

6. Continue this process of pulling the egg until there is no more uncooked egg to fill the empty space. (The reason you do this is to create texture in your omelet; it also helps decrease the cooking time by moving the layer of uncooked egg onto the pan.)

7. Once the egg layer is set in the pan add the cheese (this is the moment where you can also add sautéed vegetables or meats of your choosing).

8. Tilt the pan away from you and allow the omelet to slide up the lip of the pan, and using your rubber spatula gently fold the tilted end on top of the other.

9. Slide the omelet onto a plate—the residual heat will finish melting the cheese.

10. Salt and pepper to taste.

26 BREAKFAST

HEARTY SOUTHWESTERN BREAKFAST

1 crispy fried egg

1 packet of instant microwavable quinoa (you can sub rice for quinoa if you prefer)

½ can of black beans, drained and rinsed (pour the beans out of the can into a mesh strainer, rinse with water to remove the juice from the can)

2 pieces of thick-cut bacon, diced

2 Thai chilies, thinly sliced

2 Tbsp of white vinegar

1 Tbsp of sugar

A handful of chopped cilantro for garnish

Pinch of salt & pepper

Serves 1

1. Begin by placing the sliced chilies in a bowl, cover them with the vinegar and sugar. This is going to create a quick pickle on the chilies—the vinegar will begin to break down the cell walls of the chilies, extracting some of the raw heat and softening the pepper.

2. Place a stainless steel pan on medium heat.

3. While the pan is still cold add the diced bacon, as the pan begins to come up to temperature the bacon will begin to render.

4. Continue stirring the bacon until all the fat has rendered out, about 10 minutes.

5. Remove the bacon bits from the pan with a slotted spoon and place them on a paper towel-lined plate to drain off any excess grease.

6. Pour the bacon grease into a mug, and wipe away any remaining bacon bits in the pan to prevent burning.

7. Place the pan back on medium-high heat and pour around 1 tablespoon of the bacon grease back into the pan.

8. Add the rinsed black beans to the pan and spread them into an even layer.

9. After about 2 minutes the beans will begin to sizzle and split open. You'll get little crispy bits on the bottoms, this is perfect.

10. While the beans are cooking, in a separate pan make the crispy egg using the method instructed in the previous recipe (see page 24), the egg and the beans should finish cooking at the same time.

11. Pile everything high on top of your quinoa or rice.

12. Finish by garnishing with the pickled chilies and fresh cilantro.

13. Salt and pepper to taste.

GREEN GARDEN OMELET

3 eggs, beaten

¼ cup of broccoli florets, sliced

¼ cup of green onions, sliced

½ cup of spinach

3 Tbsp of butter

1 clove of garlic, minced (minced means to cut something up very small)

½ sliced avocado

⅓ cup shredded cheese (I use white cheddar)

Pinch of salt & pepper

Serves 1

1. Place a pan on medium-high heat, add 1 tablespoon of butter.

2. Once the butter is melted sauté the broccoli for 3 minutes or until soft and slightly browned. (The broccoli should sizzle when it hits the pan.)

3. Add the garlic to the pan and stir for 45 seconds.

4. Add in the spinach and stir until it is wilted. (This means cook the spinach until it shrivels up and clumps together).

5. Remove the veggies and wipe any remaining bits out of the pan.

6. Turn the heat down to medium and add 2 tablespoons of butter.

7. Once the butter is melted pour in the eggs.

8. Let the eggs set for around 30 seconds, then using a rubber spatula, begin to pull the layer of cooked egg from the edges of the pan slightly into the center. The egg should hold to where you pull, creating a ripple of egg.

9. Tilt the pan to move the uncooked layer of egg into the now vacant area in the pan.

10. Continue this process of pulling the eggs until there is no more uncooked egg to fill the empty space.

11. Once the egg layer is set in the pan add the cheese and sautéd vegetables.

12. When an omelet is stuffed full with veggies and meats it can be much more difficult to flip in the pan. To avoid breaking the omelete begin to slide it out of the pan onto a plate whole. Just before the final half of the omelet is about to leave the pan, flick it over the half that is on the plate.

13. Top the omelet with sliced avocado and season with salt and pepper.

COOKING BACON

Bacon, 2 slices per serving (I recommend buying uncured thick cut bacon)

Tip: Regardless of which method you use, make sure you save your bacon grease! While it is still hot pour the grease into a coffee mug. As it cools it will turn white and congeal into a solid. This can be kept in your fridge and is a beautiful replacement for butter when sautéing onions or cooking eggs to add a bit of that lovely bacon flavor.

Regardless of whether or not you decide to keep the grease, you should never pour it down the drain. It will cool and clog your pipes right up. Instead, let it cool in the mug then spoon into the garbage to discard.

There are two ways I cook bacon: in a pan and in the oven. If I am only cooking a few pieces for myself, I will cook bacon in a pan. If I am cooking for a large group of people I prefer to use the oven method. Both are very simple—let's begin with the pan.

The pan method:

1. Place the bacon strips directly into a cold pan.

2. Place the pan on the stove and turn the heat to medium. By placing the bacon in a cold pan then turning on the heat you are gently letting the bacon come up to temperature with the pan. This will slowly melt away the fat of the bacon, this is known as rendering.

3. After about 7 minutes give the bacon a flip and continue cooking for 5–7 more minutes.

4. The final cook time will depend on how crispy you like your bacon.

The oven method:

1. Preheat the oven to 400°F.

2. Get a baking sheet and line it with parchment paper or aluminum foil (this is not necessary to the cooking process but boy will it make your life easier when you go to clean up).

3. Line the bacon on the baking sheet.

4. Bake in the oven for 15–20 minutes.

NOT YOUR MOTHER'S COOKBOOK

THE POACHED EGG

While not as common of a method for cooking eggs, poaching can yield the perfect egg for an eggs benedict, breakfast sandwich, or even the finishing touch for a bowl of ramen noodles. Poaching an egg can be difficult but there are a few hacks that will take all the hassle right out of it.

1 egg

Splash of white vinegar

Pinch of salt & pepper

Serves 1

The traditional method of poaching an egg:

1. Bring a pot of water to a boil, then reduce the heat so the water is simmering just below a rolling boil.

2. Add a splash of vinegar to the water (this raises the acidity of the water which helps the egg whites stick together so they don't disperse and float all over the place in the pot).

3. Place a spoon into the water and begin to stir clockwise until the water begins to spin in the pot creating a vortex (the movement of the water forces any stray egg white particles to collide and coagulate around the egg yolk).

4. Crack the egg into a small bowl and gently drop the egg into the center of the spinning water vortex.

5. Cover the pot and let the egg poach for 5 minutes.

6. Remove the poached egg from the pot with a slotted spoon, and season with salt and pepper.

Plastic wrap

½ Tbsp of olive oil or cooking spray

1 egg

Ramekin or small bowl

Pinch of salt & pepper

The no-vinegar, no-swirling, no-hassle method:

1. Bring a pot of water to a boil, then reduce the heat so the water is simmering just below a rolling boil.

2. Line a small bowl with plastic wrap and rub it with olive oil or spray with nonstick spray.

3. Crack the egg into the lined bowl.

4. Fold up the plastic wrap tightly around the egg. Pinch the plastic wrap at the egg and twist up the access plastic wrap using your other hand. Tie the twisted ends into a knot.

5. Place the wrapped egg into the pot of simmering water. Cover and cook for 5 minutes.

6. Remove the egg and gently cut away the plastic wrap. Season the egg with salt and pepper before serving.

32   BREAKFAST

Let us now move away from eggs and over to my favorite breakfast dishes: **the sweet ones.** I'm talkin' pancakes and French toast. You may not realize it, but understanding when to flip a pancake is the same skill that will help you when searing expensive meats.

There's a misconception with pancakes that you are supposed to flip when you see bubbles. This is not true. You want to flip when the bubbles pop and leave holes in the batter. If the hole fills in with more batter it is not ready to flip. Usually, it takes around 3–4 minutes for the first side of a pancake to cook. When you go to flip the pancake it should lift up with ease; if it is sticking to the pan give it a few more minutes, it is not ready to flip quite yet.

If you are making a large batch of pancakes make sure you wipe the pan and reapply butter after every few pancakes. The butter in the pan should be a golden brown color and should never blacken. To avoid the butter blackening do not go any higher than medium heat when making pancakes.

Tip: The milk solids in butter are what burn at a high heat. Clarifying butter is a way of removing the milk solids, making butter suitable for cooking at higher temperatures. To clarify butter, simply heat up a stick of butter in a saucepan until it is melted and bubbling. The milk solids will naturally float to the surface where you can take a spoon and skim them off the top. You can also purchase clarified butter in any supermarket. You can use clarified butter in the place of vegetable oil if you want the butter flavor without the risk of it burning.

APPLE CINNAMON PANCAKES

1 cup of all-purpose flour

1½ tsp of baking powder

1 cup of milk

1 egg, beaten

2 Tbsp of sugar

1 Tbsp of cinnamon

½ tsp of nutmeg

½ of a honey crisp apple, grated

Butter for frying

Apple topping:

½ of a honey crisp apple, diced

½ cup of maple syrup

2 tsp of cinnamon

1 Tbsp of butter

Serves 2

1. In a mixing bowl combine the flour, sugar, cinnamon, nutmeg, and baking powder. Whisk until combined.

2. Pour in the milk and the beaten egg. Continue whisking until there are no visible lumps of flour in the batter.

3. Grate half an apple directly into the batter, and stir until combined.

4. Place a nonstick pan on medium heat and add in 2 tablespoons of butter.

5. Once the butter is melted and bubbling, spoon in the pancake batter.

6. Allow the pancakes to cook for about 4 minutes on the first side, flipping when the bubbles stop popping. The pancakes should flip with ease if they are ready to be flipped.

7. Cook on the opposite side for about 1–2 minutes.

For the topping:

1. Place a saucepan on medium heat and add the butter.

2. Dice the remaining half of your apple and add it to the saucepan with the cinnamon.

3. Allow the apple and cinnamon to cook in the butter for around 2 minutes or until the apple has softened.

4. Add the maple syrup.

5. Stir the mixture until the syrup has warmed up, about 1 minute.

6. Pour the warm syrup and apple mixture over your stack of pancakes.

NOT YOUR MOTHER'S COOKBOOK 35

FRENCH TOAST

3 Tbsp of sugar

½ cup of milk

4 eggs, beaten

2 tsp of vanilla extract

2 tsp of ground cinnamon

9 slices of brioche, challah, or white bread

Butter for frying

Powdered sugar for topping

Serves 2

Tip: The key to perfect French toast all starts with choosing the right bread. You want something that has loads of butter in it like a brioche or a challah loaf. I tend to stay away from the cinnamon swirl bread, especially the pre-sliced kind, when making French toast. It tends to be too thin to properly hold the batter, causing the bread to fall apart when cooking—although sometimes you can find unsliced cinnamon bread in a bakery, and this I would use. As a last resort, you can use regular white bread.

Contrary to what you might believe, stale bread works best. You want stale bread because it allows the bread to absorb more batter. The dryer the bread, the more soaking power it holds. If you know you're going to make French toast, leave the bread out the night before. If you decide to make it on a whim and don't have any dried bread, slice what you have and pop it in the oven for about 10 minutes at 200°F to dry the bread out slightly.

Growing up, I ate French toast practically every day of the week. It became the first dish I was obsessed with. I would make it for breakfast, I would make it for dessert, I would make it with berry compotes, I would make it with dark chocolate.

The point is I made it a lot, so much so that it was my go-to when I was in the dessert round of *Chopped*. I made a deep-fried French toast dipped in dark chocolate topped with macerated strawberries and champagne. French toast has the ability to be a showstopper when done right.

1. In a mixing bowl beat together the eggs, sugar, cinnamon, milk and vanilla extract until equally combined.

2. Lay the bread in a shallow tray or dish.

3. Slowly pour the batter over the bread. Let it soak for 2 minutes, then flip and soak for an additional minute. Tip the pan to ensure as much batter as possible gets absorbed into the bread.

4. If you don't have a tray simply dunk the bread directly into the bowl of batter. Hold it submerged for a bit then flip and repeat.

5. Place a nonstick pan or griddle on medium heat and melt about 2 tablespoons of butter.

6. Once the butter is melted begin to lay the bread into the pan.

7. After about 3–4 minutes give them a flip. They should flip with ease and be golden brown.

8. Cook the opposite side for an additional 2–3 minutes.

9. Serve with warm maple syrup and powdered sugar.

10. Wipe the pan and reload it with butter after every few pieces of french toast you cook.

NOT YOUR MOTHER'S COOKBOOK

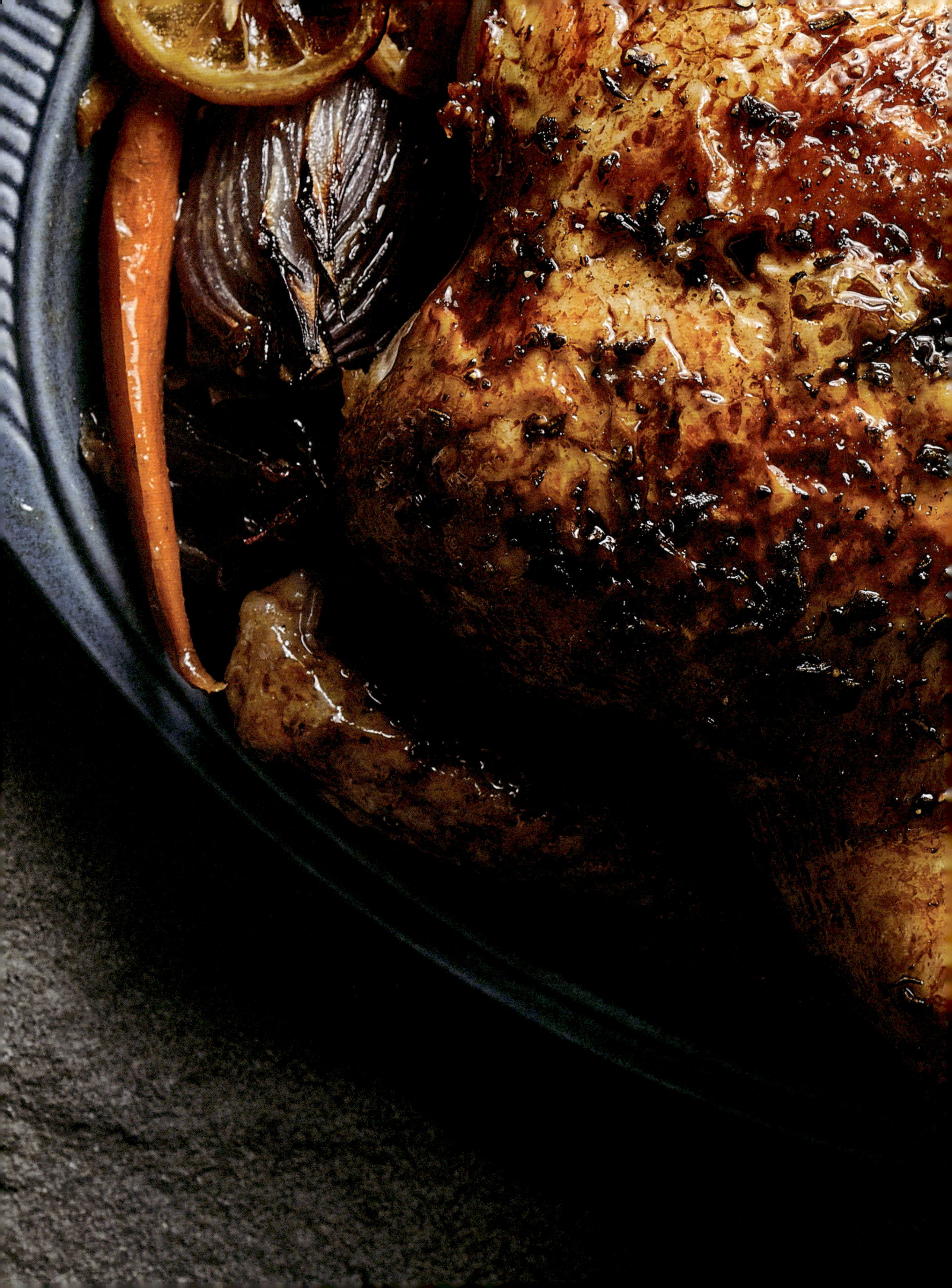

CHICKEN

Cooking chicken properly is a skill everyone should have in their arsenal. Chicken is a great protein to begin cooking with because it takes on flavor extremely well. Once you understand the basic methods for cooking chicken, it becomes a blank canvas for you to express yourself as a cook.

Chicken is also great in the sense that you only need to worry about cooking it through. Unlike other proteins, where the doneness of the meat can vary from rare to well done, chicken only has 2 options—raw and cooked. This makes it an ideal protein for building on the skill of heat control and getting a sense for when a protein is done cooking.

Much like tasting your dish as you cook, you should be actively feeling your protein throughout the cooking process. Notice how spongy a piece of chicken feels when you poke it when it's raw. Poke it when it is cooked perfectly and notice how it is firmer but still has some give. Poke it when it's overcooked and it will be very firm with no give—this is because all the moisture has been cooked out, leaving you with dry chicken.

Understanding a general sense of how food feels when it's properly cooked will help you immensely in the cooking process. I do not recommend following the time of a recipe to the exact minute. Use time in this book more as a general guideline; every stove is different, and every pan conducts heat differently than others—this all plays a factor into the cook time of a dish.

Rather than following the time to a T, use your senses of touch and sight to determine when a protein is cooked to completion. This is a skill that takes practice to develop, it won't happen overnight. Don't be afraid to slice into your chicken when you think it might be done cooking, this is how you will test your senses. The juices of the sliced chicken should run clear and it should be white throughout. Remember you can always put something back on the heat if it's undercooked—you can't do anything to save it if it's overcooked.

The three main cuts of chicken you will cook are:

- Breasts
- Thighs
- Legs & wings

The flavor varies based on the cut. If you like darker meat with deeper flavor go with the thighs, wings, and legs. If you like white meat with slightly less natural flavor go for the breast. My favorite cut is the thigh. It has a higher fat content than the breast which makes it easier to get a moist and juicy end product every time. Cooking chicken with the skin-on and bone-in will give you much more flavor than if you were to cook it with the bone-out and skin-off. The trade-off is time.

Let's begin with the easiest method of cooking chicken: pan searing.

Searing is an essential step to cooking protein. Searing builds a crust of flavor on your meat which creates a seal, locking in all the juices. You can cook a protein to completion quickly by searing it, or you can sear to build flavor then finish the cooking process later with a slow braise or roast in the oven. Whether it be for a beautiful ribeye steak or a humble chicken breast, the sear is crucial to the flavor of a dish.

To properly sear, you need your pan on medium-high heat. Get ready to hear a sizzle, and don't be afraid of oil spitting up at you, it happens. You only get one shot at creating a sear so be patient. If you go to turn your protein and it isn't pulling away from the pan with ease, wait. Don't force a flip, the crust hasn't formed yet. Wait until the protein comes off cleanly. Notice how the skill of knowing when to flip transfers over from breakfast; although you are cooking at different temperatures the same rules apply—if it sticks don't flip!

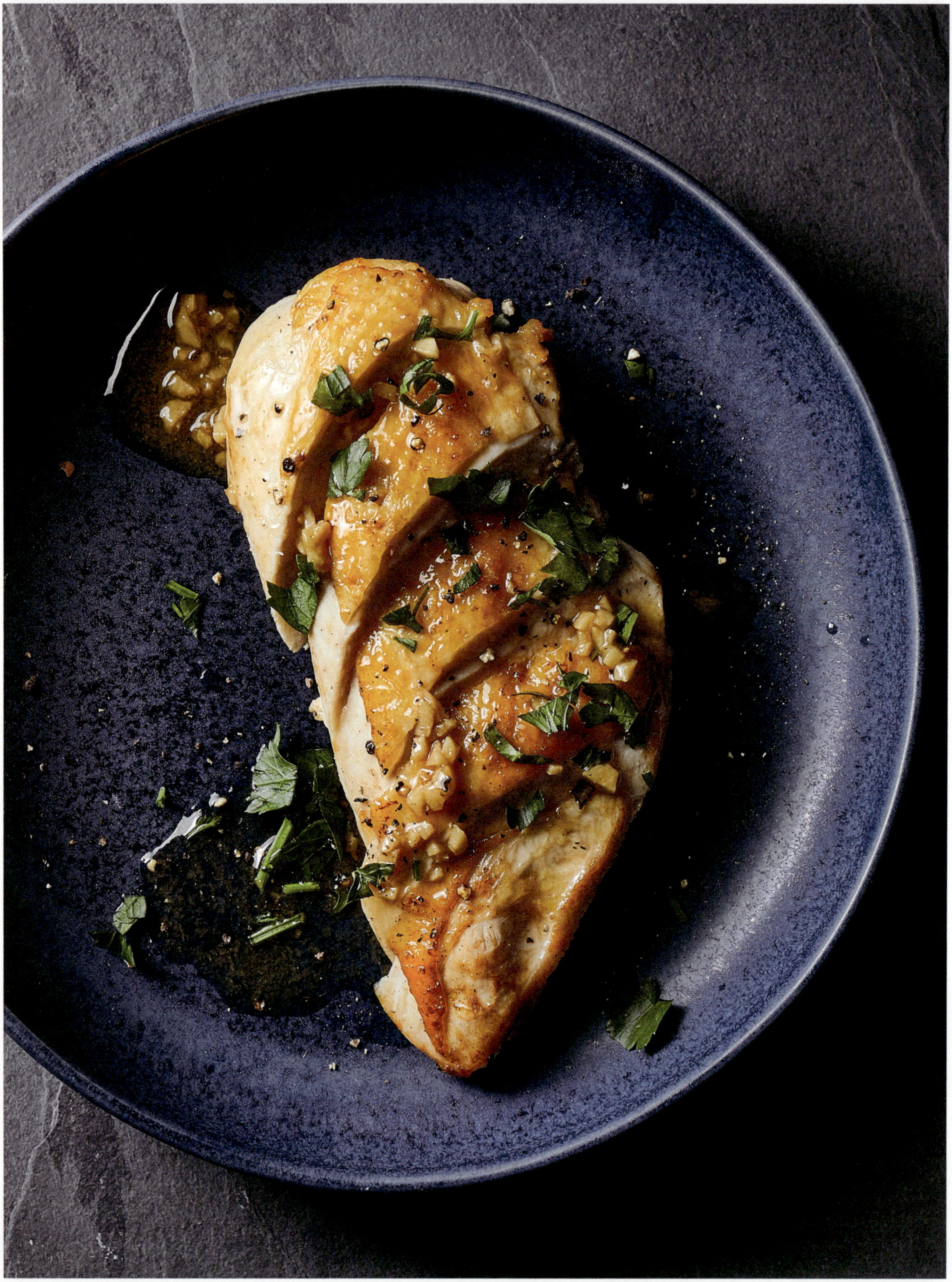

PAN SEARED CHICKEN BREAST

1 chicken breast

1 Tbsp of olive oil

Pinch of salt & pepper

Handful of fresh parsley, chopped

Serves 1

1. Begin by butterflying the chicken breast. To do so place your hand flat on top of the breast. While holding a sharp knife in your other hand, find the middle point of the breast and slice almost entirely through. Remove your hand and unfold the breast, it should look like a heart or butterfly.

2. Pat the breast dry with a paper towel. Any moisture will cause the breast to steam in the pan rather than sear.

3. Salt and pepper the breast on each side.

4. Place a pan on medium-high heat. Allow the pan to come to temperature (around 3 minutes) then add in the oil. The oil should shimmer in the pan.

5. Lay the breast in the pan, being sure to lay it away from you to reduce the risk of hot oil splashing on you. You should hear a sizzle as soon as the breast hits the pan. If you don't, that means the pan is not hot enough and you won't get a good sear. A good way to see if the pan is ready for searing is to flick some water into it before adding oil. If the water beads up and jumps out right away then you're ready to go.

6. Once the chicken hits the pan press it down evenly, then do not touch it again.

7. Allow the chicken to sear for around 3-4 minutes so a crust can form. Remember if you go to flip the breast and it is still sticking to the pan, then the sear is not yet complete. If you flip too soon, you'll end up ripping the chicken, leaving the crust (with all the flavor) stuck to the pan. Hold your horses, you'll know your sear is complete when the breast naturally becomes unstuck from the pan.

8. Once the breast is flipped, sear the other side for around 3-4 minutes. Total cook time depends on the thickness of your breast. This is where touch comes into play. Slice into the thick part, is it white all the way through? If so it is done. If not, let it cook for another minute and check again.

9. Remove the breast from the pan. Your chicken is complete!

NOT YOUR MOTHER'S COOKBOOK

QUICK PAN SAUCE

¼ cup of white wine

2 Tbsp of butter

Juice of ½ a lemon

1 clove of garlic, minced

Serves 1

You can make a very quick sauce for your chicken with minimal ingredients. Your pan should have a brown layer in the place of where the chicken was cooking, this is known as the pan *fond*. There is a ton of flavor in this and it should be taken advantage of to make a quick sauce.

1. Place the pan back on medium-high heat and allow it to come back up to temperature for 2–3 minutes. It's important to get the pan hot, but not too hot. You do not want the fond to turn black and begin to smoke. If this happens the fond is burned and the sauce will taste bitter.

2. Once the pan is hot add in the white wine and lemon juice—it should steam up immediately, if not your pan was not hot enough. (This technique is known as deglazing a pan. Deglazing is anytime you put liquid in a hot pan to scrape off the residue from searing or sautéing. Think of it like cleaning a layer of flavor off of your pan that becomes the base for a delicious sauce.)

3. With a wooden spoon begin to scrape the fond off of the pan using the moisture of the wine and lemon juice to lift it. Continue to do this for about 45 seconds or until half of the liquid has evaporated.

4. Turn the heat to medium-low and add in butter. Once the butter is melted add garlic and let it bubble in the butter until the garlic becomes fragrant and turns slightly brown. This should take around 2 minutes.

5. Turn off the heat.

6. Allow the chicken breast to rest for 5 minutes then slice it into pieces at a 45° angle.

7. Place the chicken on a plate and pour the pan sauce over it.

8. Garnish with fresh parsley.

Once you have mastered cooking a chicken breast that has been butterflied open, try cooking one whole. The cook time will be longer but the same process of searing and feeling for doneness applies. The trade off for the additional cook time is that you will be left with a more elegant looking end product on the plate.

This same searing method can be applied to boneless skinless chicken thighs. However, if using bone-in, skin-on thighs the cook time will almost double. The trade-off is you'll have more flavorful chicken. If you want to get the most fantastic crispy chicken skin on your thighs then I recommended placing them skin-side down in a cold pan. Remember when we talked about rendering bacon? Well, chicken skin acts the same way. You want to slowly introduce heat to the chicken skin so it renders and becomes crisp.

Coming up next: the method cooking for the ultimate bone-in skin-on chicken thigh.

PAN SEARED CHICKEN THIGH

1 bone-in skin-on chicken thigh

Pinch of salt & pepper

Serves 1

1. Pat the chicken thigh dry with a paper towel. Once dry, season with a pinch of salt and pepper.

2. Place the thigh in the pan with no oil or butter, the fat will render out of the skin and become the oil in your pan.

3. Place the pan on the stove and turn the heat to medium-low.

4. It may seem like nothing is happening but trust me it is, be patient, and don't touch your chicken. After about 3–4 minutes you will start to hear a sizzle.

5. Let the thigh continue to cook like this on a low heat for 15–20 minutes. You will know when to flip it because the skin will release from the pan signifying that it has gone crisp.

6. Once the thigh is flipped, turn the heat up to medium-high.

7. Cook the thigh skin side up for about 5–8 minutes if cooking with the bone in. If the bone is out your cook time on this side will be around 2–3 minutes.

CHICKEN ALFREDO PASTA

1 seared chicken breast

8 oz of fettuccine noodles

Alfredo sauce (page 132)

Serves 2

1. Sear the chicken breast as previously instructed (page 43).

2. Cook the pasta according to the packet instructions.

3. Toss the pasta in the alfredo sauce.

4. Top the pasta with the sliced seared chicken.

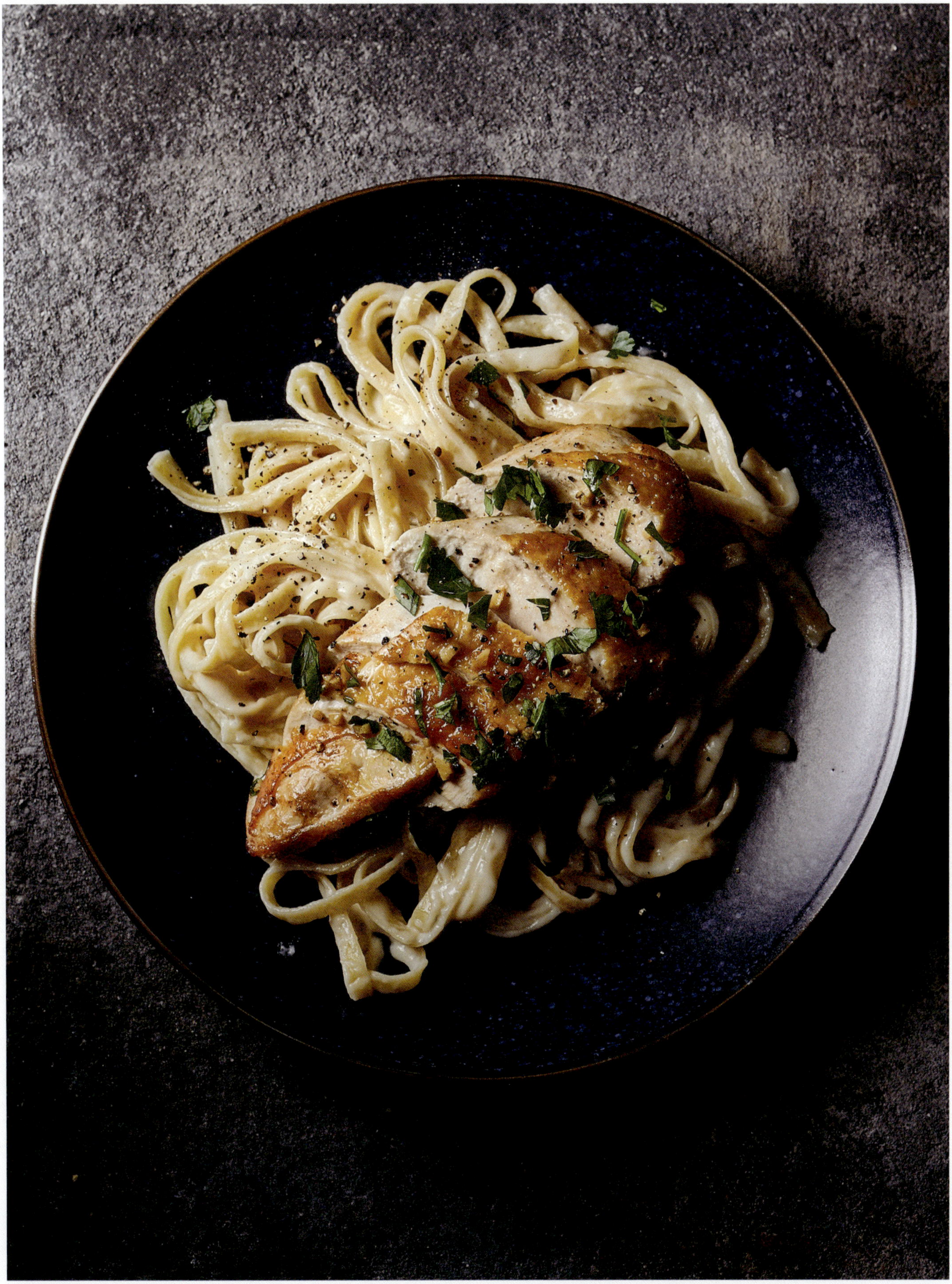

CHICKEN STREET TACOS WITH CHARRED PEACH SALSA

1 seared chicken breast

½ tsp of cumin

2 tsp of chili powder

2 flour or corn tortillas

½ cup of salsa (page 142)

Serves 2

1. Before pan searing the chicken breast, season it with cumin and chili powder in addition to the salt and pepper.

2. Sear the chicken as previously instructed (page 43).

3. Heat the tortillas over an open flame or wrap them in tin foil and place them in a 200°F oven for 10 minutes.

4. Dice the seared chicken into half-inch cubes.

5. Fill the warm tortillas with diced chicken and top with salsa.

CHICKEN CAESAR SALAD

1 seared chicken breast

1 large bowl of salad mix

¼ cup of croutons

¼ cup of shaved parmesan for garnish

Caesar salad dressing to coat the salad evenly (page 141)

Serves 2

1. Sear the chicken breast as previously instructed (page 43).

2. Toss the salad with the dressing.

3. Dice the seared chicken breast into half-inch cubes.

4. Combine the chicken with the salad mix.

5. Top the salad with shaved parmesan and croutons.

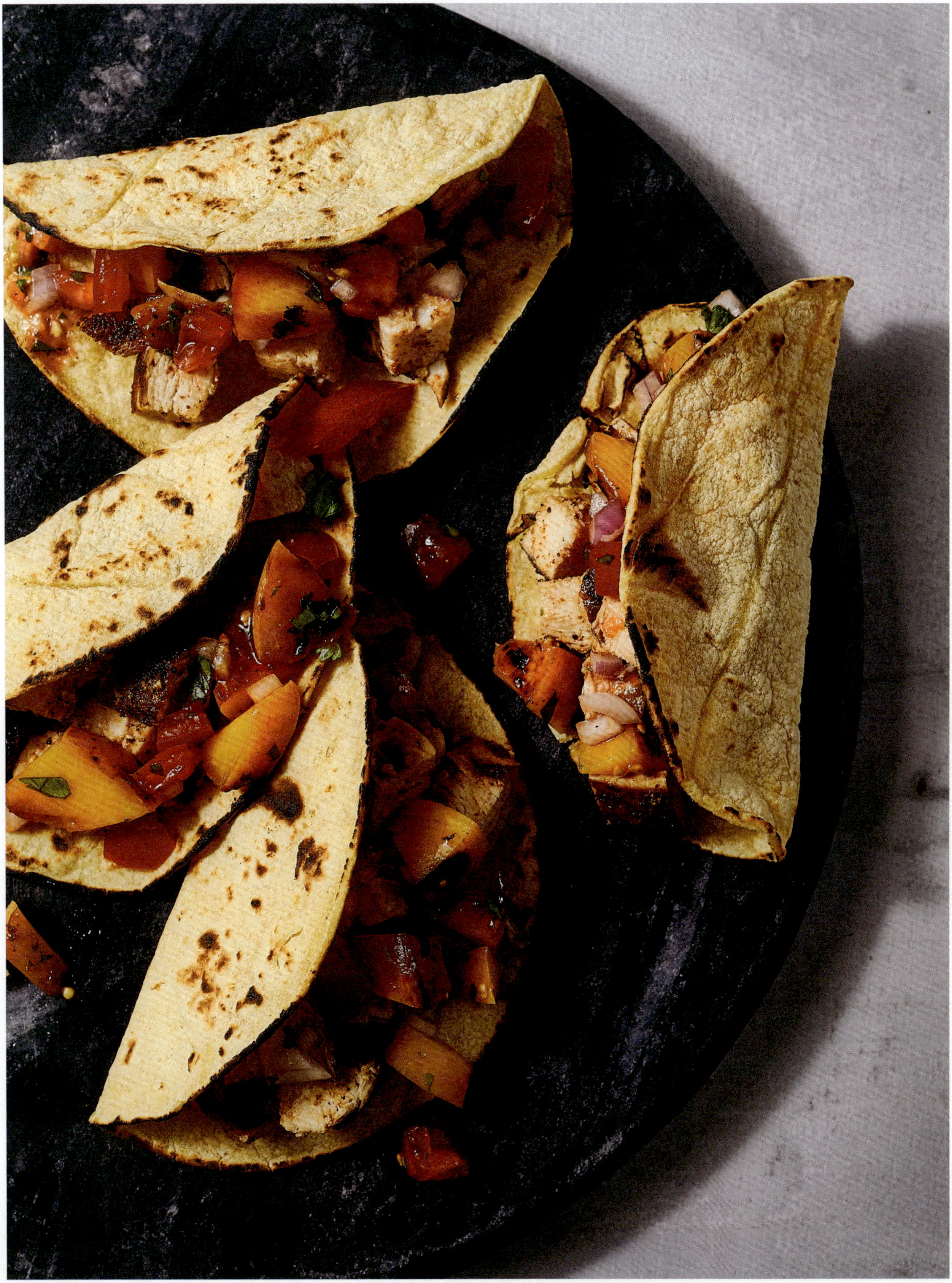

Let's continue to build off the technique of **searing.** In the following recipes, you'll notice that you begin cooking the chicken with an initial sear. Then, by adding some liquid to the pan, the chicken will finish cooking by either simmering in the liquid or through steaming by covering the pan with a lid. These are very easy one-pan dishes where you will create large flavors with minimal effort, and it all stems from the initial sear.

ONE PAN HONEY MUSTARD CHICKEN

2 Tbsp of olive oil

4 boneless skinless chicken thighs

¼ cup of beer (a nice lager is ideal)

1 Tbsp Dijon mustard

2 Tbsp honey

1 Tbsp of hot sauce

3 cloves of garlic, minced

Fresh parsley, minced (about half a bunch)

Pinch of salt & pepper

Serves 2

1. Season the chicken thighs with salt and pepper.
2. Place a pan on medium-high heat and add the olive oil.
3. Place the chicken thighs in the pan and press down lightly.
4. Do not touch the thighs for 3–4 minutes.
5. Flip the thighs once they have no resistance in the pan, meaning a sear has formed.
6. Cook the thighs on the opposite side for 2 minutes.
7. After 2 minutes add the minced garlic to the pan and sauté for 45 seconds then pour in the beer.
8. Mix the mustard, honey, and hot sauce together until combined, then add the mix to the pan after the beer.
9. Stir everything until combined then simmer for 2–3 minutes. (Your total cook time should be around 8–10 minutes for the chicken to cook through.)
10. Place the chicken on a plate and pour over the sauce. (If the sauce is too loose you can thicken it by placing the pan back on medium-high heat and simmering the sauce for about 5 minutes until it reduces down, or by adding a slurry (see page 128 to learn more about slurries).
11. Garnish the chicken with fresh parsley to serve.

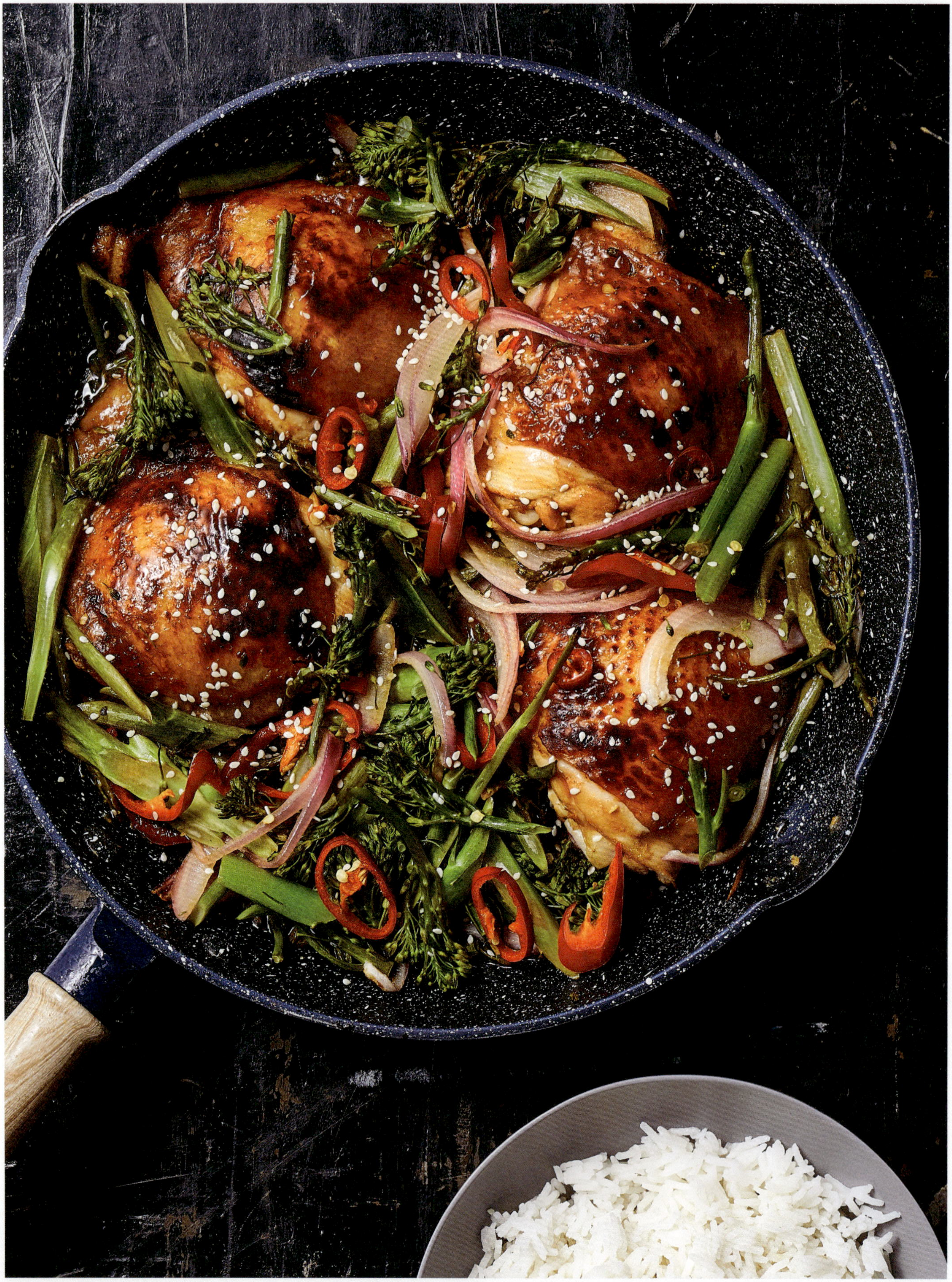

ONE PAN STICKY ASIAN CHICKEN

4 bone-in skin-on chicken thighs

¼ cup of soy sauce

¼ cup apple cider vinegar

3 Tbsp of honey

¼ cup of water

½ Tbsp of hot sauce

2 cloves of garlic, minced

1 Tbsp of ginger, minced

4 heads of broccoli rabe, sliced

1 red onion, sliced

1 red chili pepper, sliced

Pinch of salt & pepper

Sesame seeds for garnish

Serves 4

1. Season the chicken thighs with salt and pepper then place them in a large mixing bowl.

2. To that bowl add in the soy sauce, vinegar, honey, and hot sauce. Stir until everything is combined and set aside.

3. Slice the stalks of the broccoli rabe on a slight bias so you have roughly 1–2 inch pieces. Break the florets apart into individual pieces.

4. Thinly slice the red onion and red pepper (slightly angle your knife when slicing the red pepper so you get thin obtuse slices rather than perfectly round ones).

5. After the chicken has had about 20 minutes to soak in the marinade, pat the thighs dry but do not rinse the marinade off.

6. Place a pan on medium-high heat and allow it to come to temperature for 3 minutes. Once the pan is hot lay the thighs in the pan skin side down.

7. Cook the thighs for 3 minutes or until the skin is golden and releases from the pan. (You aren't as worried about crispy skin here because you are going to steam the chicken which will take away any crispness. You will crisp up the skin at the very end by putting the pan under a broiler).

8. Once the chicken thighs are flipped add the veggies to the pan and pour in ¼ cup of water as well as the remaining marinade.

9. Cover the pan and reduce the heat to medium.

10. Leave the pan covered on the stove for about 10 minutes to finish cooking the chicken through.

11. While the chicken is cooking place your broiler on high.

12. After 10 minutes take the cover off the pan and place it under the broiler for 5 minutes to crisp up the skin. The skin should begin to bubble and char slightly.

13. Remove the chicken and veggies from the pan and reduce any remaining liquid by placing the pan back on the stove top and simmering. You have the option to use a slurry to thicken the sauce here as well (for more on slurries, see page 128).

14. Pour the pan sauce over chicken and garnish with sesame seeds.

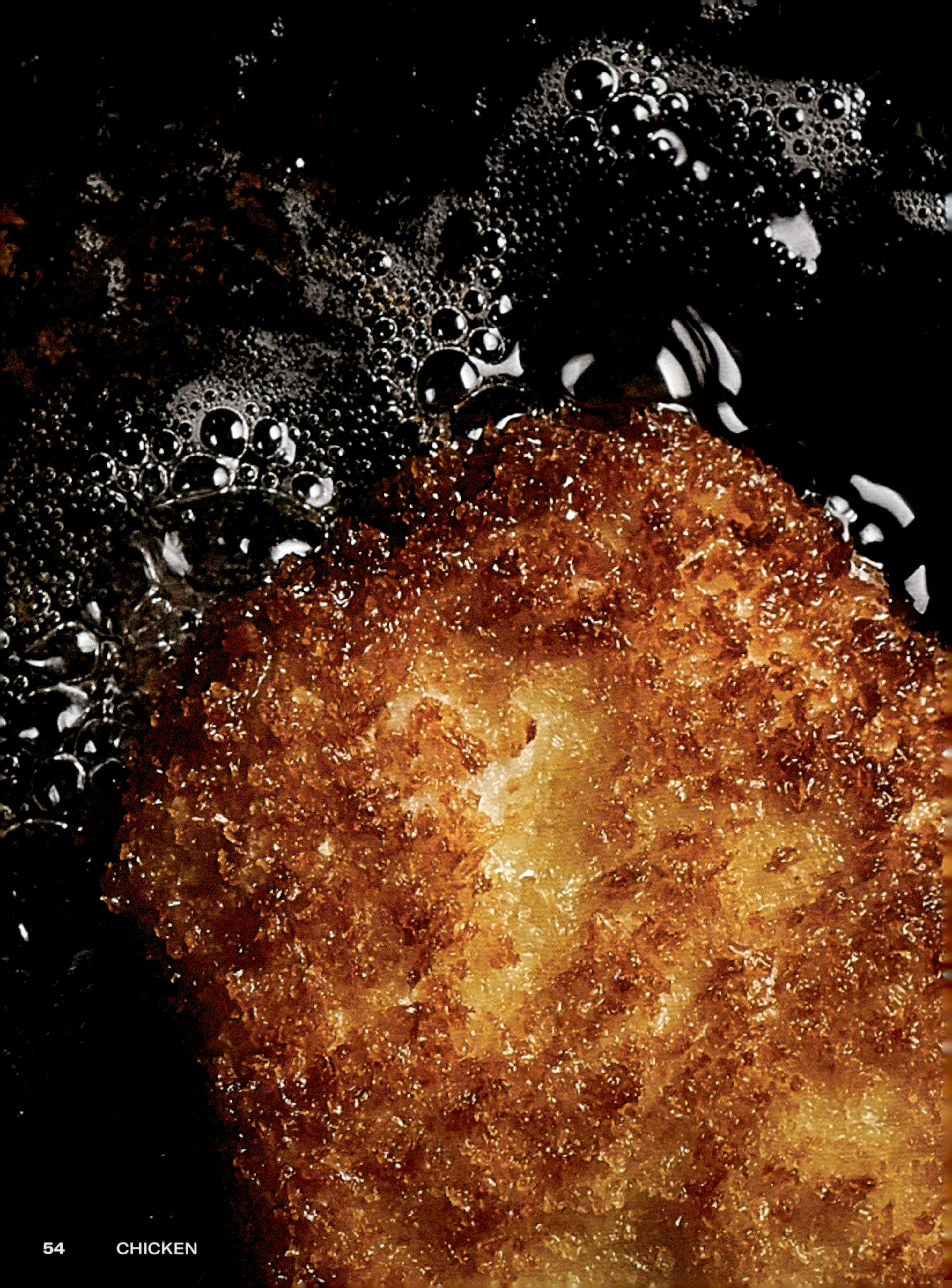

Much like searing, when you **pan fry** you are cooking whole proteins to completion in just one pan on the stovetop. The difference with pan frying is the amount and type of oil you use. When you sear you are using the direct heat of the pan to cook your protein; when you pan fry you are using the heat of the oil. When pan frying you always have at least a quarter of an inch of neutral oil in the pan. A neutral oil is an oil with no strong flavor and a higher smoke point, meaning it will not burn at high heat—some examples are vegetable oil, soybean oil, and canola oil. Olive oil can be used for pan frying, as you did with the ultimate fried egg, however, it is less typical because it will add a strong flavor to the food and will begin smoking when left on the stove for a prolonged period of time. Unless specifically stated in the recipe do not use olive oil for pan frying.

A crucial aspect of pan frying is the breading process. Rarely will you pan fry without first breading your protein in some fashion. To bread something is to coat first with flour, then dip in beaten eggs, and finish by rolling in crushed breadcrumbs, cereal, or your favorite cracker to create, you guessed it, a breading. You can take this breaded protein and either pan fry, deep fry, or bake it in the oven to create a crispy crust around your protein.

NOT YOUR MOTHER'S COOKBOOK

CHICKEN

PAN FRIED CHICKEN BREAST

1 chicken breast

¼ cups of breadcrumbs

¼ cup of all-purpose flour

2 eggs, beaten

Pinch of salt & pepper

Oil for firing (vegetable, soybean, canola)

Serves 1

This is the basic method for pan frying a chicken breast. The exact same method can be applied to a chicken thigh. In this case, use skinless chicken thighs. Due to the breading, the chicken skin will not have direct contact with the oil so it will not go crispy, rather it will steam underneath the breading and yield a rubbery tough texture. You can fry a chicken thigh with the bone in if you'd like, just know that, as when searing with the bone in, the cook time will increase.

1. Pour the flour onto a plate and season it with salt and pepper.

2. Place the breadcrumbs on a separate plate.

3. Beat the eggs into a shallow dish or plate.

4. Trim any fat/skin off of the chicken breasts (the white parts).

5. Slice the chicken in half horizontally as if you were butterflying, only this time slice all the way through to create two pieces. To decrease the cook time you can pound the chicken to make it even thinner. If you would like to do this I recommend covering the chicken in plastic wrap and pounding it with a mallet or the palm of your hand until the breast is a quarter of an inch in thickness.

6. Place a pan on medium-high heat and fill it with around ¼ inch of oil.

7. Allow the oil to come to 350°F. This will take about 10 minutes on medium-high heat. (The temperature of the oil can be tested by flicking in some of the breadcrumbs. What you want to see is for them to begin to bubble instantly. They should begin to turn golden, if they turn black instantly and start to smoke your oil is too hot. In that case, remove the pan from the heat for 5 minutes then test again.)

8. Dredge the chicken pieces in the flour (to dredge means coat lightly).

9. Transfer the floured chicken to the egg dish and roll until fully covered with egg.

10. Transfer the chicken from the egg to the breadcrumb plate, and turn until fully coated with breadcrumbs.

11. Fry the chicken in the oil for around 3 minutes. You're looking for the breading to turn golden brown. Check the chicken by lifting it slightly with tongs. Once you have that golden brown color, flip and fry for an additional 2 minutes on the other side (time will vary depending on thickness).

NOT YOUR MOTHER'S COOKBOOK

PAN FRIED CHICKEN SANDWICH

1 pan fried chicken thigh, cooked as previously instructed (For this recipe I use cornflakes in the place of breadcrumbs, but you can use either.)

1 slice of pepper jack cheese

1 potato bun

½ Tbsp of butter for toasting the bun

4 pickles

Sauce:

2 Tbsp of mayonnaise

1 Tbsp of barbeque sauce

½ Tbsp of Dijon mustard

½ Tbsp of honey

Serves 1

For the ultimate chicken sandwich, pan fry a chicken thigh. If you want a deli-style chicken cutlet then cover your thigh in plastic wrap and bash it until it is about a ¼-inch thick. This will decrease cook time by about a minute on each side.

1. Pan fry the chicken as previously instructed (page 57).
2. Set the oven broiler to high.
3. Pace a slice of cheese on top of your pan fried chicken thigh.
4. Broil in the oven for 2–3 minutes or until the cheese is melted and bubbling.
5. Combine the ingredients for the sauce in a bowl and stir.
6. Toast the bun in a pan with butter.
7. Spread the sauce on the bun, top it with pickles and the pan fried chicken thigh.

CHICKEN PAILLARD

1 pan fried chicken breast pounded to ¼ inch in thickness

A handful of arugula

¼ cup of parmesan cheese

The zest of 1 lemon (to zest is to finely grate the outer layer of the lemon)

2 Tbsp of parsley, minced (or 1 Tbsp of dried parsley)

Serves 1

1. Pan fry the chicken as previously instructed (page 57). The only difference with this method is you will be adding the parmesan, lemon zest, and parsley to your breadcrumb mix for when you coat the chicken.

2. Serve the chicken topped with arugula and a fresh squeeze of lemon.

CHICKEN PARMESAN

1 pan fried chicken breast

Tomato sauce (page 132)

8 oz of fresh mozzarella

½ of cup fresh parmesan, grated

Serves 1

This method does not have to be limited to chicken. Simply swap out the chicken breast for eggplant, and using the same steps you'll have an eggplant parmesan. Replace the chicken thigh with a pork cutlet and you have yourself the base for a Japanese Katsu Sandwich (page 62).

1. Pan fry the chicken breast as previously instructed (page 57).

2. Set the oven broiler to high.

3. Place the pan fried chicken on a baking sheet.

4. Cover the chicken with a heavy spoon full of tomato sauce.

5. Lay the fresh mozzarella over the sauce.

6. Top everything off with freshly grated parmesan cheese.

7. Place the tray in the oven and broil on high for 5 minutes or until the cheese is golden and bubbling.

NOT YOUR MOTHER'S COOKBOOK

JAPANESE KATSU SANDWICH

2 pork loin steaks, pounded to ½ inch in thickness

½ cup of all-purpose flour

½ cup of panko bread crumbs

2 eggs, beaten

1 cup napa cabbage, sliced

4 slices of white bread

Vegetable oil for frying

Pinch of salt & pepper

Tonkatsu sauce:

1½ Tbsp oyster sauce

2 Tbsp of Worcestershire sauce

2 Tbsp of ketchup

1 Tbsp of soy sauce

2 Tbsp of brown sugar

½ Tbsp of honey

Serves 2

1. If the pork loin is not already sliced thin, pound it out until it's about half an inch thick.
2. Season the flour with salt and pepper.
3. Bread the pork as you learned previously by dredging first in flour, then rolling in the beaten egg mixture, and finally in panko.
4. Heat the vegetable oil in a pan on medium-high heat for 10 minutes.
5. Pan fry the breaded pork for 3 minutes or until golden brown, then flip and fry the opposite side for 2–3 minutes or until golden brown.
6. In a bowl combine the oyster sauce, Worcestershire, ketchup, honey, and brown sugar. Stir until the sugar is dissolved.
7. Thinly slice the cabbage and cut the crust off of your bread.
8. Coat each slice of bread with the sauce, then top with cabbage, and finally the fried pork cutlet.
9. Slice the sandwich into thirds and enjoy.

NOT YOUR MOTHER'S COOKBOOK 63

We've gone over pan frying and searing; let us now move on to roasting and baking. Although often used interchangeably the difference between roasting and baking comes down to two major factors; food structure and oven temperature. Technically we associate baking with foods that lack a solid structure before entering the oven (think doughs, cake batters, cookies, etc.). Baking is done at a lower temperature, typically not higher than 375°F. Roasting, on the other hand, always occurs above 400°F and is associated with foods that have a solid structure prior to entering the oven (think meats and vegetables). That really doesn't matter to what I am about to teach you. All you have to know is that roasting chicken yields rich flavor with crispy charred skin and juicy tender meat.

I get very excited about the idea of roasting a chicken whole. There's something about it that feels primal—you are cooking in a way that hasn't changed since man invented fire. Sure the technical aspect of an oven has evolved over time, but the method of cooking an animal whole remains the same. To this day the best roasted chicken I've ever had was in Nepal in a tiny village deep in the Himalayan mountain range. I was invited to the village as a guest of two guys my age I met while aimlessly wandering around Kathmandu; they explained to me that I was the first westerner to visit their village and for that, they were preparing a special dinner. I was given the honor of cutting the head off of their chicken. The village women then cleaned it and roasted it in a clay oven with a ton of spices. The small mud kitchen, which doubled as a dining room, was filled with a deep aroma of spices and flavors. As the juices dripped from the chicken onto the hot coals steam would rise and make your stomach growl with hunger.

This same feeling is achieved when roasting whole chicken at home. Your house will be filled with a delightful smell and whoever you are cooking for will be drawn to the kitchen, eagerly awaiting the removal of the golden bird.

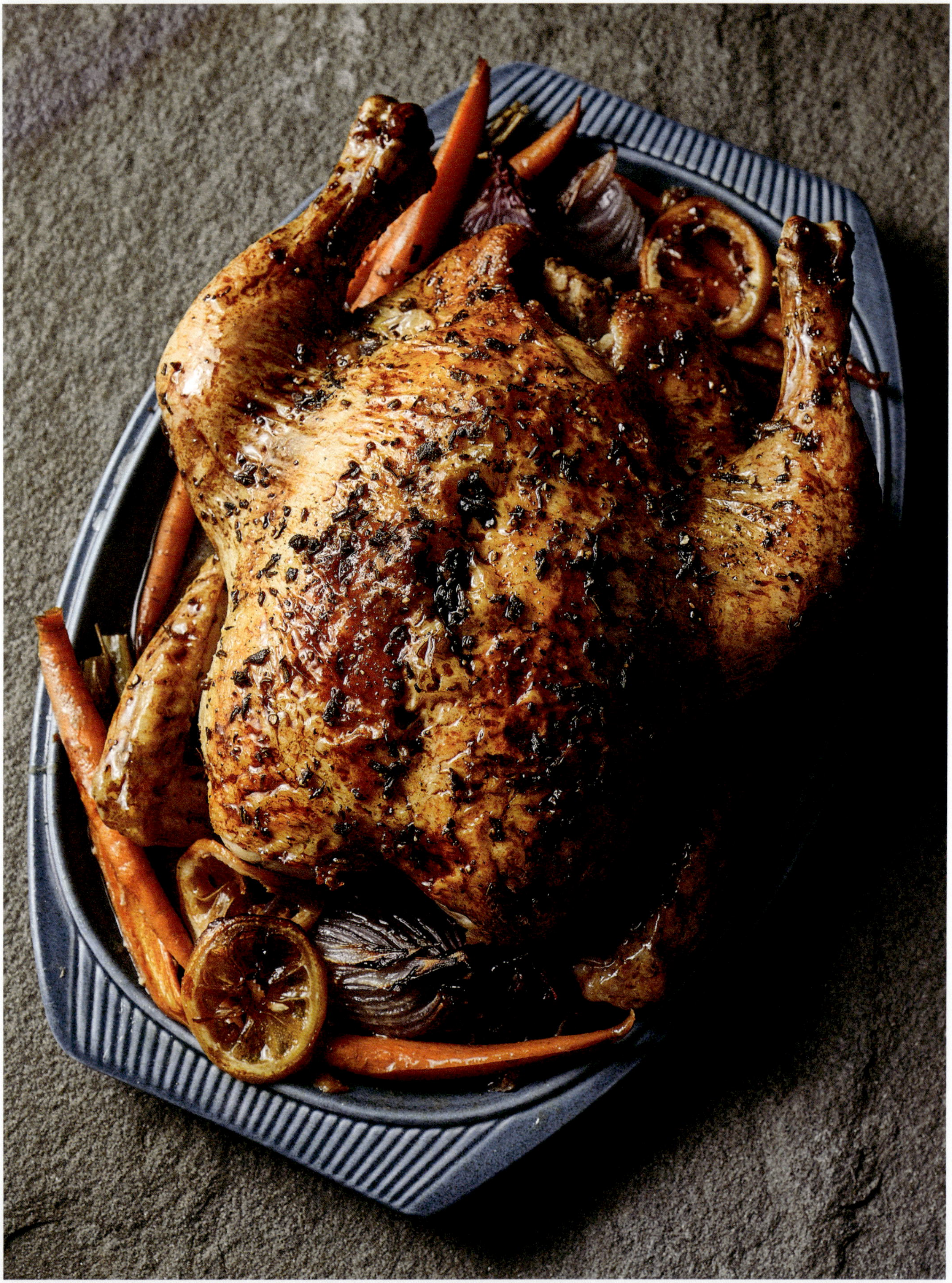

WHOLE ROASTED CHICKEN

1 whole chicken

Fresh herb bundle (thyme, rosemary and sage)

2–3 onions, quartered (It doesn't matter what kind of onions they are.)

2 carrots, cut into thirds

1 bulb of garlic, sliced in half (This is the entire root of garlic with all the cloves in it.)

1 lemon, sliced into rounds

3 Tbsp of olive oil

½ a stick of softened butter

Pinch of salt & pepper

Serves 4

Tip: If you're buying the herbs prepackaged, look for an herb pack called 'poultry seasoning' and use the entire bundle. If you're buying the herbs individually use about 3 sprigs of rosemary, 3 sprigs of thyme, and a handful of sage leaves.

1. Begin by preheating the oven to 420°F.

2. Finely chop the herbs and place them in a bowl. (Remember to remove the herbs from stocks and stems before chopping).

3. Combine the oil with the chopped herbs and a pinch of salt and pepper. Stir until a paste forms.

4. Rub the oil and herb paste all over the skin of your chicken.

5. Using your fingers, enter the bird through the neck and gently pull the skin off of the breasts creating a cavity.

6. Stuff the top of the breasts with the remaining oil-herb paste and half a stick of softened butter.

7. Gently rub your hands along the outside of the breasts to work the butter down.

8. Slice a lemon and place it in the cavity of the bird (do not overstuff, use about 2 slices).

9. Place the bird on a roasting tray over the quartered onions, garlic, carrots, and the remaining lemon slices. You should have enough vegetables to cover the bottom of the roasting tray if not just cut up some more. Any root vegetable will suffice. This will act as a bed for your chicken, allowing air to get underneath the chicken to ensure even cooking.

10. Roast at 420°F for 1 hour. You can check to see if the bird is done by poking a knife in the space between the thigh and the drumstick. If the juices come out clear the chicken is done. If they come out pink and cloudy then continue cooking.

11. Transfer the chicken to a cutting board to carve.

12. Don't throw away all the leftover vegetables and juices in the pan! You can use those to make an awesome gravy.

(Continued on next page)

NOT YOUR MOTHER'S COOKBOOK

Gravy:

1. Start by making a roux in a saucepan. Combine 2 tablespoons of butter with 2 tablespoons of flour and whisk the mixture over medium heat for 5 minutes (see page 128 to learn more about rouxs).

2. Once the roux is formed, pour in 1 cup of the juices from the roasting tray, keeping the vegetables out.

3. If you have a fine mesh sieve, pour the vegetables into that over the saucepan and press them into the sieve with a spoon. All the wonderful flavor from the roasted vegetable will be pushed through the sieve and will take your gravy to the next level.

4. Simmer the gravy and stir for 5 minutes or until the gravy has thickened.

5. Add a pinch of salt and pepper.

Carving a whole chicken:

1. Begin by finding the breast bone in the middle of the chest of the bird.

2. Once you feel that with your knife, slice down on an angle to both the right and the left of the bone to remove the breasts.

3. To remove the wings and drumstick, find the knuckles, place your knife on top of them and slam down with force.

BUFFALO CHICKEN SLIDERS

1 whole roasted chicken, shredded (you can also use a store-bought rotisserie chicken)

¾ cup of Frank's RedHot

2 Tbsp of ranch dressing

½ a packet of ranch seasoning

½ a cup of butter, melted

⅓ cup of blue cheese and mozzarella to top

1 packet of mini dinner rolls or King's Hawaiian bread

Serves 4

1. Preheat the oven to 350°F.
2. Combine the melted butter with half a packet of ranch seasoning. Mix the melted butter, ranch dressing, and Frank's RedHot in a bowl (reserve about 1 tablespoon of butter to brush on buns before baking).
3. Add the shredded chicken to the mixture and stir until combined.
4. Slice the buns in half so the top buns and bottoms are separated but do not pull the buns apart into individual units.
5. Line a roasting tray with the bottom layer of buns. Layer on the chicken mixture and top with cheese. Cover with the top layer of buns.
6. Brush the top of the buns with the remaining butter mixture.
7. Bake for about 10–15 minutes at 350°F or until the cheese is melted and buns are golden.

COLD CHICKEN SALAD SANDWICH

Leftover roasted or rotisserie chicken, shredded (about 1 cup for 1 sandwich)

1 stalk of celery, diced

2 green onions, sliced

2 Tbsp of mayonnaise

1 Tbsp of spicy chili sauce or any kind of hot sauce

½ tsp of curry powder

Pinch of salt & pepper

New England-style hot dog bun

Serves 1

1. Mix all the ingredients together in a bowl until combined.
2. Stuff the bun full of the chicken salad mixture.
3. If you have leftover chicken skin from the roast I like to fry it up in a pan until crispy then break it up and use it as a topping for the sandwich.

CHICKEN

FIVE INGREDIENT FAJITAS

4 chicken breast, sliced into ¼-inch thick pieces

3 bell peppers, thinly sliced

4 Tbsp of vegetable oil

2 red onions, sliced

½ packet of taco seasoning

6–8 tortillas

Serves 4

Tip: If you wuld like to make the taco seasoning yourself. mix together 2 teaspoons chili powder, 2 teaspoons cumin, and 2 teaspoons paprika.

Let's conclude the chicken portion of this book by making a simple one-pan chicken fajita bake. This is perfect if you are trying to feed a group of people with minimal prep work and clean up.

1. In a large mixing bowl toss the sliced chicken, onions, and peppers with the oil and half a packet of taco seasoning until everything is evenly coated with oil and spice.

2. Place the mixture on a cooking tray, being sure to spread everything out in an even layer (if the ingredients are stacked on top of each other they will steam rather than roast).

3. Roast in the oven at 425°F for 25–30 minutes.

4. Serve the roasted chicken and vegetables in warm tortillas with a squeeze of lime.

NOT YOUR MOTHER'S COOKBOOK

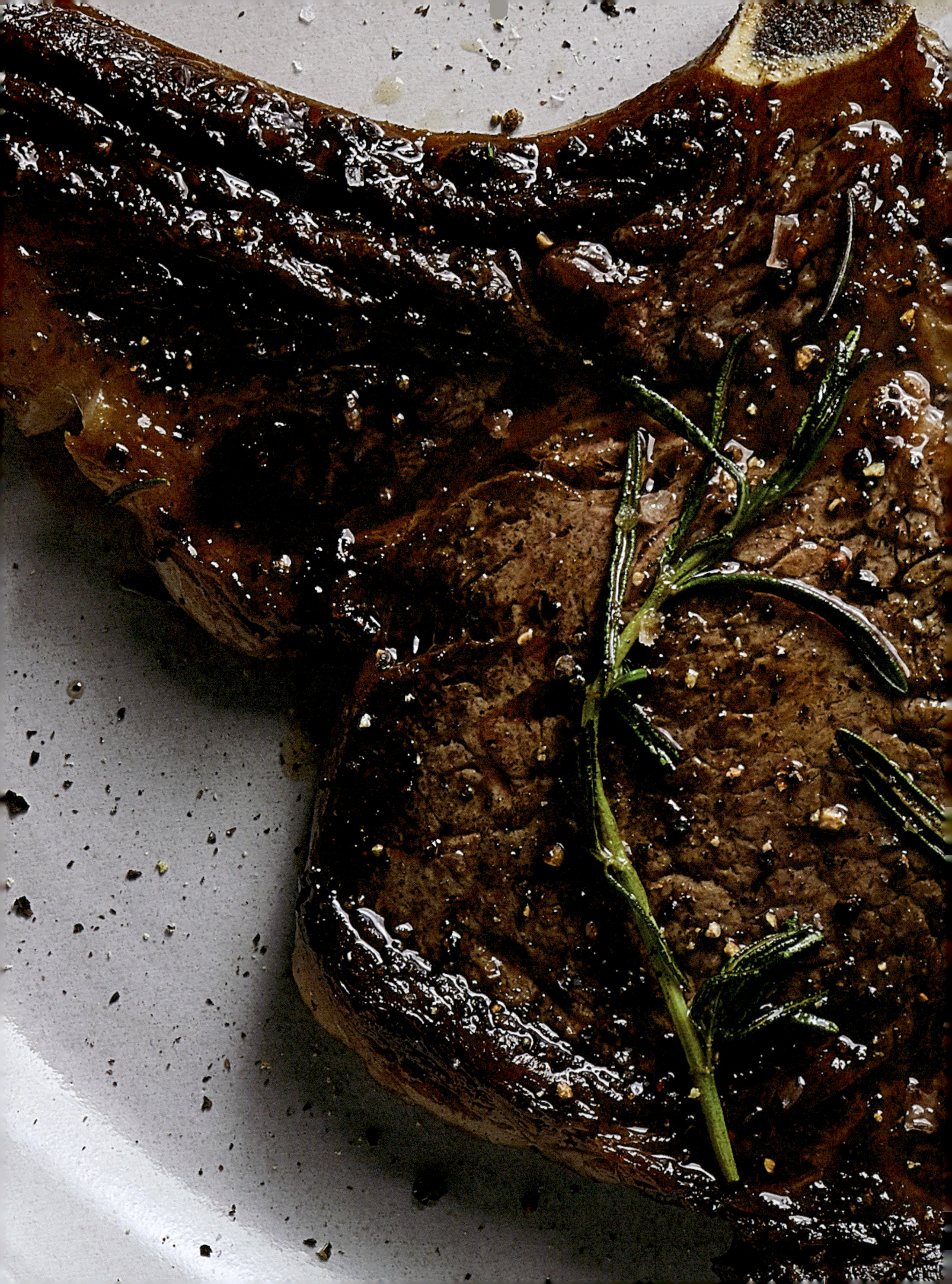

BEEF

Now that you have mastered chicken, let's take it up a notch. Let's talk beef, motherfucker. Unlike chicken, beef has a much wider range of cuts and each one requires a slightly different technique for cooking. The key to cooking beef is knowing what type of cut you have. If you have a cheaper cut you might need a marinade to help take some of the toughness out, or you might need to braise the beef low and slow to break down all the connective tissue. If you have an expensive cut all you'll need is a quick sear on high heat.

In this section of the book I'll cover the same basic techniques of searing and pan frying, only this time I'll introduce a new technique known as braising. To braise food is to cook it partially covered in liquid on a low simmer. Braising is how you turn those cheap cuts of meat into melt-in-your-mouth flavor bombs. I'll go more in-depth on braising in a second. Let us first begin with pan searing beef and for that there's no better place to start than with steak.

Cuts such as fillet mignon, ribeye, strip, sirloin, and T-bone (which is just a strip steak and tenderloin attached by a bone) need nothing more than a sear to cook. These cuts are a gift to mankind and should be treated accordingly. These cuts will never require a marinade or a special seasoning and there is no need to ever cook these steaks over medium-rare. Absolutely none. I understand some people like their steak cooked well done. If that is the case please keep it to yourself, a man can only take so much heartbreak in his life.

Other cuts such as flank, skirt, rump, hanger, tips, and flat iron require a bit more prep work to achieve the desired bite. The trade-off is they are more affordable. If prepared right they are equally as delicious, and as always they should be enjoyed at a perfect medium-rare.

Searing steak is slightly more technical than searing chicken. However, it begins with the same basic principles.

Take your steak out of the fridge and set it on the counter at least 30 minutes before you begin to cook. You do this to bring the steak to room temperature. Think of your steak like an Olympic sprinter getting ready for a race. If they were to go right into sprinting without first warming up their muscles would tighten up and they would get injured. The same thing applies to a steak—after all, it is a muscle. If you put a steak in a pan without first letting it warm up it will tighten up and go tough, leaving you with a chewy steak rather than one that hums in your mouth.

Now, as you learned in chicken, you must pat the steak dry with a paper towel to remove any moisture, giving yourself the best setup for a perfect sear. Once your steak is dry, salt and pepper it thoroughly. Do this about 5 minutes before you're going to sear—if you let a salted steak sit out too long the salt will begin to draw moisture from inside the steak to the surface, which will negate the towel dry you just did and cause your steak to steam rather than sear when it hits the pan. Olive oil can be used to sear a steak (it may begin to smoke but this is fine). If you are concerned with the smoke you can use vegetable oil or clarified butter to sear.

How many times should you flip a steak? There is not one answer to this question. It comes down to the steak you are cooking. For the purposes of this book I am assuming you will be cooking steaks on the cheaper side. These are usually no more than an inch thick and require only one flip. However, let's say you are cooking a 3-inch thick ribeye. In that case, I would recommend following my general instructions for searing a steak, then once each side is seared continue to flip it every minute or so until the steak is cooked to your desired temperature.

When searing a steak that has a fat cap on its side be sure to sear that side as well by holding the steak on its edge in the pan with a pair of tongs. If this fat cap is left unseared it will be tough and chewy when eating. However, when the fat cap is seared it will render and melt into the pan, adding more flavor for when you go to baste your steak and creating an ideal texture for when you eat it.

Always slice your steak against the grain (in the opposite direction of the muscle fibers)—if you do not do this, your steak will be gamey and harder to chew. This is because when you slice with the grain the muscle fibers remain intact. Slicing against the grain is much more crucial on tougher cuts with more pronounced muscle fibers such as a flank, hanger, or skirt steak. On tender cuts, such as the fillet mignon, this is not crucial, but it's a good habit to form. The direction in which the grain is running should be easy to detect. The muscle fibers form little groves you can see and feel, and usually run lengthwise across the steak. (Think of grains in wood, it's the same concept.)

PAN SEARED STEAK

1 steak fillet (I recommend a sirloin for beginners)

2 Tbsp of olive oil

3 Tbsp of butter

Pinch of salt & pepper

Add-ons: (not required for the basic recipe but I highly recommend)

1 whole clove of garlic

1 spring of rosemary

½ cup of red wine

Serves 1

1. Allow the steak to come to room temperature by letting it sit out for 30 minutes prior to cooking.

2. Salt and pepper the steak thoroughly.

3. Place a pan on medium-high heat and allow it to come to temperature (around 3 minutes).

4. Make sure the pan is hot, flick some water into the pan. It should bead up and jump instantly.

5. Add 1 tablespoon of oil to the pan, it should begin to shimmer.

6. Lay the steak into the pan and, as with any sear, do not touch it for at least 3 minutes so a crust can form.

7. After about 3 minutes use tongs to flip the steak. It should be unstuck from the pan when you flip, if not the steak is not finished searing.

8. Once flipped, sear on the opposite side for around 3 minutes.

9. This is where feeling your food comes into play. I can't see the steak you are cooking. I have no idea how thick it is which makes it hard for me to give you an exact cook time. Press your finger into the steak and see how it responds. A general guide to gauging how cooked a steak is is to compare the feeling of the steak to the palm of your hand. Press into the meaty part of your hand where the thumb meets the palm; this is a general feel for rare. Now slide your finger down a bit towards your wrist; this is medium-rare. Now press where your palm meets your wrist; this is well done. Your steak should never feel like this.

10. In the final minute of cooking add the butter, garlic, and rosemary to the pan with a splash of olive oil. (You add the olive oil to raise the specific heat of the butter, keeping it from burning.) Not much oil is required, you want all the flavor from the butter. The garlic does not need to be chopped, simply press down on it with the flat side of your knife to break it open slightly. The same goes for the rosemary, throw the whole spring in unchopped.

11. Let the garlic and rosemary blister away in the pan for around 30 seconds.

(Continued on next page)

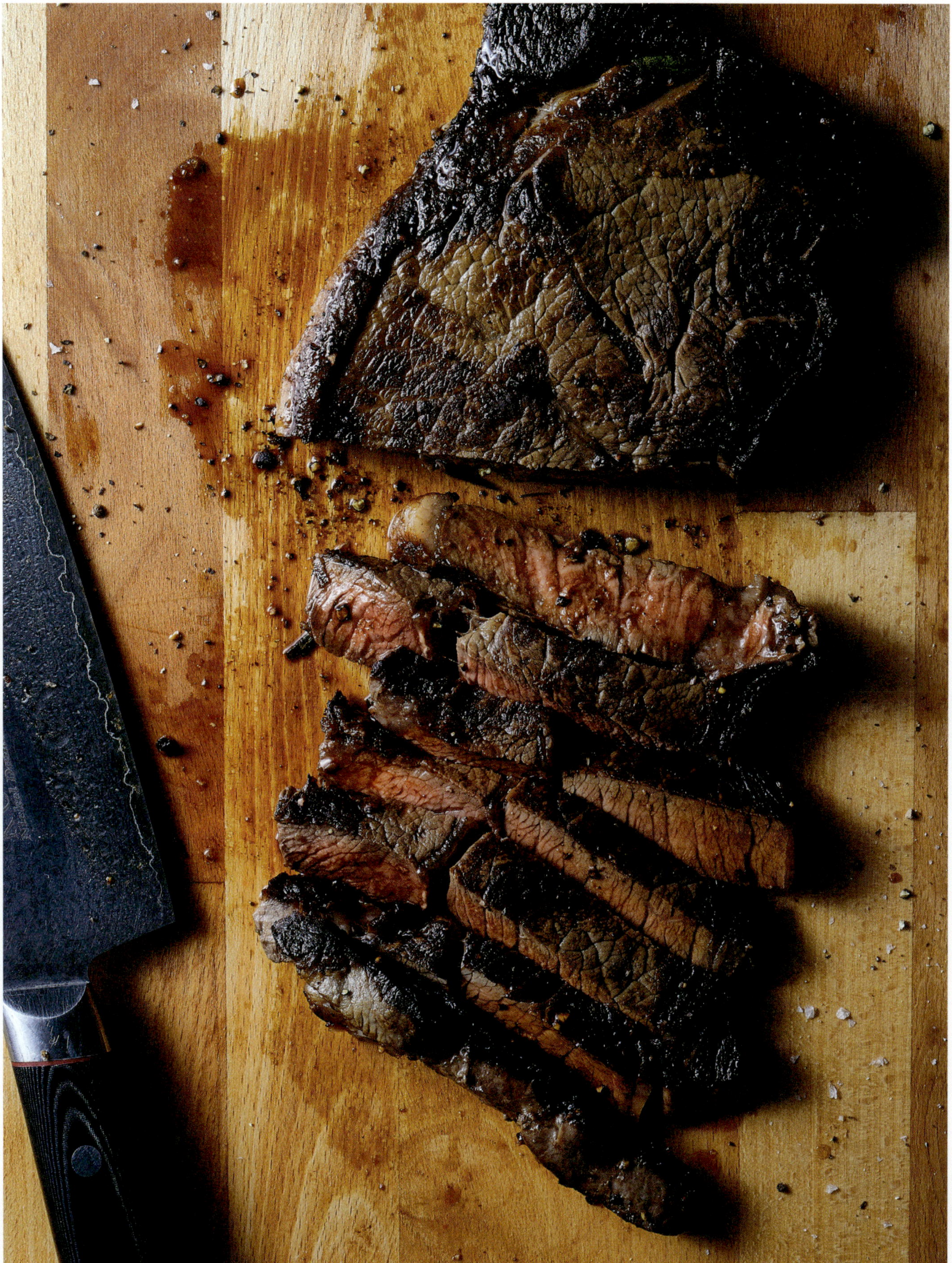

Tip: To baste is to pour liquid or pan dripping over food during the cooking process. This adds flavor and, in the case of long roasts in the oven, helps keep the protein moist.

12. Tilt the pan towards you and use a spoon to baste the butter on top of the steak.

13. After about 30 seconds of basting remove the steak from the pan and allow it to rest for 5 minutes before slicing into it. Resting is a crucial step in the cooking process. What resting meat does is it allows for all the juices inside the steak to redistribute into the meat. If you cut in too early all those wonderful juices will flow out of the steak, and all your hard work will have been for nothing.

14. While the steak is resting, pour any remaining juices and butter from the pan over it.

Quick pan sauce:

1. To make a quick pan sauce, place the pan back on medium-high heat and let it come back up to temperature (about 2–3 minutes on the heat will do this).

2. Once hot, deglaze the pan with red wine and scrape the fond with a wooden spoon. (You should be familiar with these terms, if not see the previous chapter or glossary.)

3. Reduce the wine down to about half of what you originally poured in. (Notice how this is the same process you used when making a pan sauce for chicken only with red wine. A general rule of thumb when making pan sauces is use white wine for chicken and fish, and red wine for beef and pork.)

4. Take the pan off the heat and, stirring constantly, begin to add small cubes of cold butter (2 tablespoons in total). Stir until the butter is melted and fully incorporated. You want to use cold butter in this instance because the cold butter melts slowly, which will allow for more stable emulsification between the fat of the butter and the water content of the wine. If you were to use warm or melted butter the emulsification would be unstable and the sauce is likely to split (meaning you would have a layer of butter floating on top of the wine).

5. Once the steak has rested, slice it at a 45° angle and pour the pan sauce over it to finish.

6. Serve with roasted vegetables (page 150).

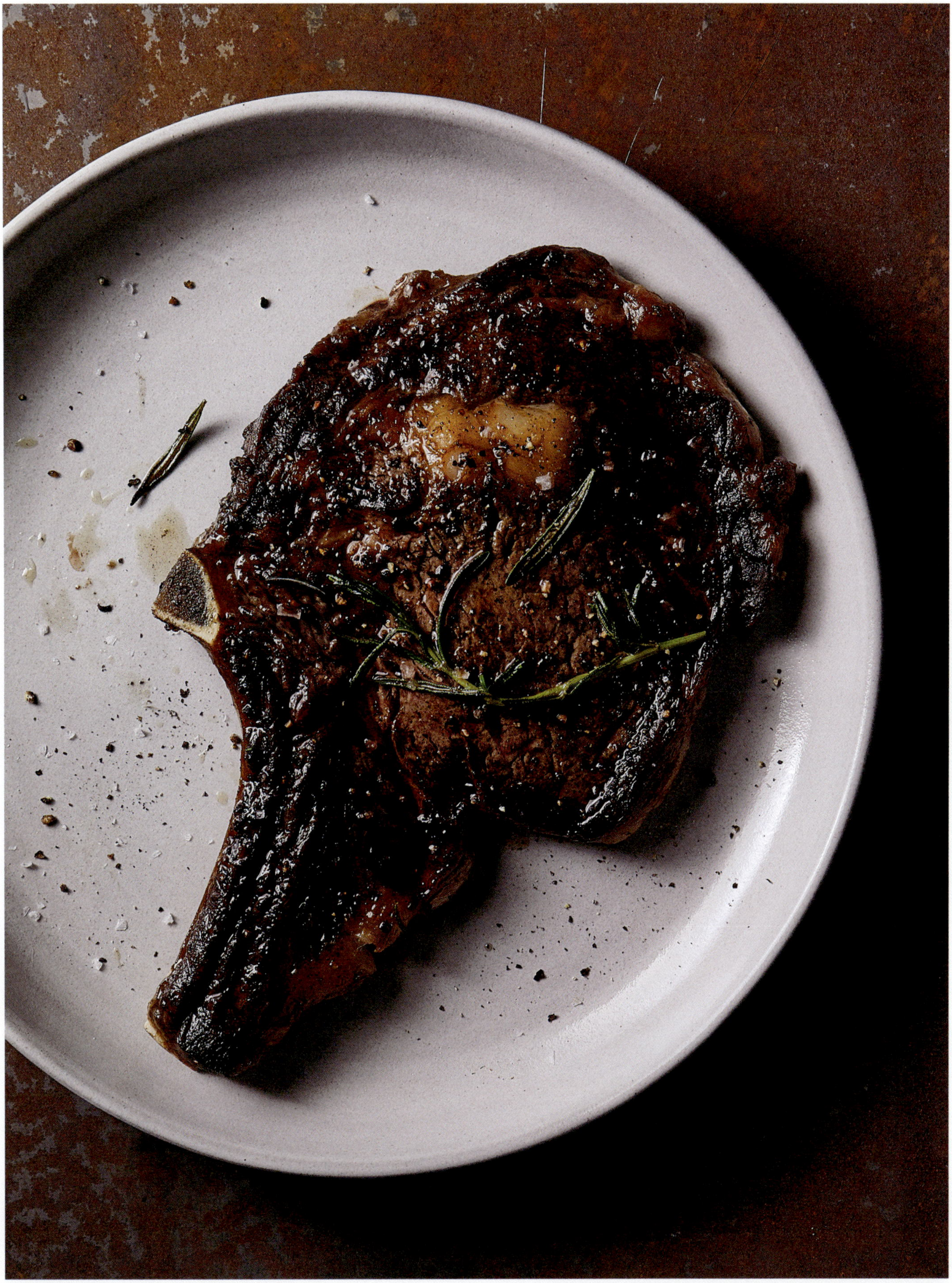

CLASSIC BURGER

6 oz of ground beef

½ Tbsp of vegetable oil

1 Tbsp of butter

A slice of cheese of your choosing

Pinch of salt & pepper

Bun

Serves 1

The key to a perfect burger is all in the type of ground beef you use. You want there to be enough fat in the burger—this not only adds flavor but also keeps the burger juicy. When buying ground beef you'll see on the packaging label a number that signifies the fat to lean meat ratio. Look for a number that says 80/20 (this means that there is 20% fat to 80% lean meat). This is a solid ratio for a burger.

1. Roll the ground beef into a ball, then press it down between the palms of your hands to form a patty. It should be around half an inch in thickness.

2. Next, take your thumb and press it into the center of the patty, this will help the burger keep a flat shape while it cooks. Meat shrinks when cooking and begins to curl, this indentation will help counteract that.

3. Once the patty is shaped, salt and pepper each side.

4. Place a pan on medium-high heat and add the butter and vegetable oil.

5. Place the patty in the pan, dimple side up.

6. As with any sear, you should hear a sizzle as soon as the burger hits the pan.

7. Cook the burger for 3 minutes on the first side, then flip using a spatula.

8. For medium-rare cook on the following side for around 4 minutes. Again this becomes more of a general guideline rather than a hard time. Look and feel to determine doneness.

9. When there is one minute left in the cooking process top the burger with cheese, and add a splash of water to the pan and cover it. The steam from the water will melt the cheese perfectly so you are left with an even layer of oozing sticky cheese.

10. Serve on a toasted bun with toppings of your choice.

NOT YOUR MOTHER'S COOKBOOK

BEEF

SMASH BURGER

8 oz of 80/20 ground beef (4 oz per patty)

1 potato bun

4 slices of American cheese

1 Tbsp of ketchup

1 Tbsp of mayonnaise

½ Tbsp of pickled relish

Pinch of salt & pepper

Serves 1

Personally, this is my favorite way to cook a burger. It cooks fast, you don't need to worry about cooking it to a specific doneness, and you get tons of gnarly crispy bits of meat held together by gooey American cheese. This style of burger is what you would find at your Shake Shack, In-N- Out, Culvers, and other popular burger joints.

1. Loosely pack the beef into 4 oz balls. You'll be using 2 balls of beef to make 1 SMASH burger.

2. Preheat a pan on medium-high heat.

3. Place the balls of beef into the pan (with no butter or oil).

4. Smash all the way down on the beef balls with a spatula until they are thin (don't worry if they break up a bit, this is where you'll get all those gnarly crispy bits. Your cheese will help hold everything together).

5. Once smashed, salt and pepper the patties.

6. Cook for 2 minutes then flip (make sure to get all the way underneath the meat, scraping hard with a spatula to ensure you get all of the crust up).

7. Once flipped, top each patty with 2 slices of cheese.

8. After about 1 minute, stack one patty on top of the other in the pan. Add a splash of water to the pan and cover for 30 seconds to melt all the cheese.

9. Remove the burger from the pan.

10. In a small bowl mix together mayonnaise, ketchup, and relish.

11. Smear the sauce on a lightly toasted bun, stack with pattys, smash on the top bun and enjoy.

BEEF

CHEESESTEAK

8 oz steak, thinly sliced (I use ribeye)

1 Tbsp of olive oil

1 yellow onion, sliced

1 red chili pepper, sliced

1 clove of garlic, minced

A few slices of provolone cheese

Pinch of salt & pepper

1 large hoagie or torpedo roll

Serves 1

This cheesesteak recipe makes for a killer sandwich with relatively minimal effort. You can splurge and use an expensive cut of beef such as a ribeye but because you are slicing the meat so thin and cooking it through, a cheaper cut like a flank steak will work just fine.

1. Throw the steak in the freezer an hour prior to cooking, this will get it nice and firm so you can slice it super thin with ease.

2. Thinly slice the steak (remember to slice against the grain).

3. Slice the onion, pepper, and garlic.

4. Place a pan on medium-high heat with a glug of olive oil.

5. Once the pan is hot, throw in the sliced onions and peppers and begin to sauté. Don't put the garlic in yet to avoid burning it (garlic cooks much faster than other vegetables which is why you often see it being added last in recipes).

6. After about 3-4 minutes or when the onions are translucent and turning brown add in your steak and thinly sliced garlic.

7. Cook for an additional 3 minutes or until the steak changes color and is cooked through.

8. Top the pepper and steak mixture with cheese. Cover and steam for 30-45 seconds or until the cheese is melted.

9. Pile everything high in a warm hoagie roll and get ready to eat.

Alright, I feel as if we have covered our bases when it comes to searing beef, let's move on to pan frying. Much like chicken, you will be **pan frying beef** in a neutral oil as well as breading it. However, the method of breading I'm about to show you is slightly different than what you did with the chicken. Rather than dredging in flour, eggs, and breadcrumbs, you will be coating your beef with corn starch. This will in turn yield a thinner coating that will add a crispness to the beef without creating a thick outer layer of breadcrumbs. My favorite beef dish to pan fry is Mongolian beef.

Then we'll move on to some tougher cuts of beef that require a little more love and care to transform. You've seen me use flank steak now in a few recipes. In my opinion, it's the best bang for your buck. However, simply searing it straight up in a pan is not the best way to prepare it. The flank is the abdomen of the cow, and therefore it is a tougher muscle. In the previous methods you sliced the flank steak thin and cooked it through so the toughness of the meat was not a concern. Now I will be teaching you how to cook the flank steak whole, and for that, you will need to do some work.

You need to break down all that muscle and connective tissue within the steak. You will do that through tenderization and marination. When you marinade you use a mix of acid and oil to tenderize and flavor a protein. This process can be anywhere from 30 minutes to 24 hours. I have found marinades to be most effective at the 12-hour mark. If you marinate for too little time, you don't reap the benefits of infused flavor and tenderized meat. However, if you marinate for too long, you can over-tenderize your meat and be left with a mushy, unsavory texture.

MONGOLIAN BEEF

12 oz flank steak

⅓ cup of cornstarch or enough to coat each piece of steak evenly

3 cloves of garlic, minced

1 thumb-sized piece of ginger, peeled and minced (ginger can be peeled easily by scraping the skin with a spoon)

3 whole dried chilies (you'll find these in the produce section next to dried fruit. Don't worry if you can't find them, they aren't crucial to the dish.)

5 green onions, sliced on a bias

Vegetable oil for frying, enough to fill the pan ½ an inch in depth

Sesame seeds for garnish

Stir fry sauce:

¾ cup of brown sugar

⅓ cup of soy sauce

1 Tbsp of hot sauce

Serves 2

Mongolian Beef is a classic American-Chinese food dish. The crispy pieces of fried beef smothered in a sweet and spicy sauce will leave you wanting more. Once you make this dish, you'll have no need to order Chinese takeout again!

1. Slice the flank steak in half lengthwise leaving you with 2 slices of steak. Now thinly slice those two strips against the grain at a 45° angle creating small thin strips of steak.

2. In a mixing bowl combine the sliced steak with corn starch. Keep adding cornstarch until all the steak is evenly coated.

3. Fill a pan with a half-inch of vegetable oil and place it on medium-high heat. Allow the pan to heat up for around 10 minutes.

4. Gently lay the cornstarch-coated pieces of steak into the oil and fry for 3 minutes or until the steak turns golden brown.

5. Remove the steak from the pan and place it on a plate lined with paper towels to drain.

6. Mince the garlic and ginger, set aside.

7. In a bowl combine the sugar, soy sauce, and hot sauce. Stir until the sugar is dissolved.

8. Place a wok or large pan on high heat. Add 2 tablespoons of vegetable oil to the wok or pan, and add the whole chilies.

9. Fry the chilies until they turn black. What this will do is add spice to the oil, giving the dish an added layer of heat. Once the chilies are blackened remove them from the oil.

10. Add the garlic and ginger to the pan or wok, stir constantly. These will cook fast, so keep a close eye on the garlic.

11. As soon as the garlic turns a light brown add in your fried steak.

12. Pour in the sauce and stir.

13. Let the pan bubble away for 1-2 minutes until the sauce reduces and get sticky.

14. Once the sauce is reduced, stir in the sliced green onions and top with sesame seeds.

15. Serve with rice.

BEEF

MARINATED FLANK STEAK

16 oz flank steak fillet

½ cup of soy sauce

½ cup of Worcestershire sauce

¼ cup of rice wine vinegar (can sub white vinegar)

¼ cup of olive oil

2 Tbsp of hot sauce

1 Tbsp of honey

Juice of 1 lime

3 cloves of garlic, minced

1 Tbsp of fresh ginger, minced

4 green onions, sliced

1 tsp of chili flake

½ tsp of salt

½ tsp of pepper

Serves 4

This recipe was passed along to me by my uncle. It's the first steak I ever learned how to cook, and it's packed full of flavor. It can be pan seared, grilled, or broiled. Broiling is a method of cooking where you use direct heat to cook. Ovens have a 'broiler' which is an exposed coil pumping constant heat directly onto what you are cooking. Broiling is effective for steaks like the flank where it can be too large to fit into a single pan. This marinade works extremely well for making steak tacos.

1. Add all the marinade ingredients in a mixing bowl and stir until combined.

2. Begin by trimming the grizzle off of the steak (this is the whitish gray shit on the steak).

3. To properly trim, get a sharp knife and begin the peel up the grizz with your free hand while gently scraping at it with your knife. Once it begins to come off you should be able to peel it away without the knife. Using a paper towel to grip the grizz will help with the process since it can be slippery.

4. Cutaway any fat (the white bits) hanging around the edges of the steak. Fat inside the steak is great, especially on the premium cuts, but when it is isolated on its own in large chunks on a cut like the flank it is best to remove it. This fat will become chewy and will make the meat difficult to eat.

5. Once the steak is properly trimmed, tenderize it by stabbing it repeatedly with a fork on each side. This will not only help break up the connective tissue inside of the steak, but it will also allow the marinade to penetrate deeper into the meat.

6. Place the tenderized steak in a large ziplock bag and pour the marinade over it.

7. Store the steak in the fridge for 12 hours, remove 30 minutes prior to cooking.

8. Do not rinse off the marinade before cooking—this will remove all the seasoning and flavor from the surface. However, you should lightly pat the steak dry with a paper towel before cooking.

(Continued on next page)

9. When you go to cook the steak, follow the same method for pan searing you learned previously (page 76).

10. This steak also cooks up great on a grill. The same techniques from pan searing apply to grilling. Treat your grill surface as if it were your pan.

11. If the steak is too large to fit into a frying pan or you do not have a grill I would recommend broiling it.

12. To do so, set your broiler to high and let it heat up for a few minutes. Place the steak on a sheet tray or directly onto the oven rack and broil on each side for about 3–4 minutes for medium-rare.

13. Once the steak is rested, slice it against the grain. Remember this is very important for flank steak because the muscle fibers are very pronounced, you need to slice across those to break them up, failing to do so will yield an extremely chewy and inedible steak.

BEEF TERIYAKI

16 oz skirt steak fillet

½ cup of soy sauce

½ cup of sake (sake is a Japanese beverage made from fermenting rice)

⅓ cup of mirin (mirin is very sweet sake used for cooking, it can be found in any supermarket in the global foods section)

1 Tbsp of sugar

⅓ cup of apple juice

Serves 4

Tip: If you do not have soy sauce, sake and mirin on hand, you can sub them out for 1⅓ cup of pre-made teriyaki sauce

The skirt steak is a cut of beef that is great to marinade. I love to use it when I make beef teriyaki.

1. Combine the soy sauce, sake, mirin, sugar, and apple juice, and stir until the sugar is dissolved.

2. Pour the marinade over your steak and seal in a ziplock bag, store in the fridge for 12 hours.

3. Take the steak out of the fridge 30 minutes before cooking to allow it to come to room temperature.

4. Pat the steak lightly with a towel but do not rinse it.

5. Heat a pan on medium-high heat or set a broiler to high.

6. Place the steak in the pan or under a broiler, do not touch it for 3 minutes.

7. After about 3 minutes flip and cook for 3–4 additional minutes for medium-rare.

8. Remove the steak from the pan or oven and let it rest for 5 minutes.

9. Slice the steak on a 45° angle against the grain and serve.

You learned that a marinade can turn a tougher cut of steak into one that explodes in your mouth with flavor—but what about the really tough cuts of beef? I'm talking about the beef shanks, the short rips, the oxtails, and the round. These cuts of beef come from the parts of the cow that are the most exercised and therefore are packed full of connective tissue. These cuts of beef, when cooked properly, can become more flavorful than any of the tender cuts. However, a marinade will not suffice to get these to an edible level, so what do you do? You fucking **braise.**

To braise means to cook food partially covered in liquid on a low simmer. Braising is how you turn those cheap cuts of meats into melt-in-your-mouth flavor bombs. This is where searing comes into play; a good sear on your protein is crucial to a successful braise.

You build off the fond in the pot from your sear, sometimes adding vegetables, then deglaze the pot with a liquid such as wine, stock, or beer. You then place your seared protein back into the pot and add more cooking liquid until the protein is almost fully submerged. You then bring the liquid to a simmer and cover the pot. Your braise is then either finished in an oven at a low temperature (between 275–335°F) or over low heat on the stove. When braising the cook time is generally around 2–3 hours, but it varies depending on the cut. You remove the lid of the pot for the final portion of the braise to allow the cooking liquid to reduce into a sauce.

Braising is hard to fuck up, but the trade-off is that it can be time-consuming. The connective tissue in these tough cuts of meat has to slowly melt away and turn into gelatin. However, there is a shortcut. I recommend that everyone has an Instant Pot pressure cooker in their kitchen. It can turn a 2-hour braise into 20 minutes.

BRAISED SHORT RIBS

5 lbs of bone-in beef short ribs

2 Tbsp of olive oil

½ Tbsp of salt

½ Tbsp of black pepper

2 Tbsp of tomato paste

1 yellow onion, diced

2 cups of red wine

2 cup of beef stock

Serves 5

Tip: The exact same method of braising short ribs can be applied to braising beef chuck or beef shanks. Swap out the short ribs for chuck and follow the exact same steps. You may need to adjust the amount of beef stock used—you should be using enough to almost cover the beef.

1. Season the short ribs with salt and pepper.

2. Heat a large pot over medium-high heat and add the oil. Allow the oil to come to temperature (2–3 minutes).

3. Place the shorts ribs in the oil and sear them until they have a deep brown crust on all sides, about 7 minutes. If you can't fit all the short ribs in the pot at once then sear in separate batches.

4. Transfer the short ribs to a plate and set aside.

5. Reduce the heat to medium and add the onions. Stir the mixture every now and then until the onions turn golden brown, about 5 minutes.

6. Add the tomato paste and stir until it gives off a sweet aroma, about 1 minute.

7. Add the red wine and stir with a wooden spoon to scrape up the fond on the bottom of the pot.

8. Simmer the wine for about 3 minutes to cook off some of the harshness from the alcohol and to reduce.

9. Add the short ribs back into the pot along with any juices that might have been released when resting.

10. Pour in enough beef stock to nearly cover the short ribs. If some ribs are poking up flip them so the bone is up and the meat is facing down.

11. Bring the pot to a simmer, then cover and place it in an oven at 325°F for 2½ hours or until the short ribs fall apart when picked at with a fork.

12. Remove the short ribs from the pot and bring the liquid up to a simmer to reduce it into a sauce.

13. Serve the short ribs warm with roasted vegetables (page 150).

INSTANT POT SHORT RIBS

5 lbs of bone-in beef short ribs

2 Tbsp of olive oil

½ Tbsp of salt

½ Tbsp of black pepper

2 Tbsp of tomato paste

1 yellow onion, diced

½ cup of red wine

½ cup of beef stock

Serves 5

You can make this same dish using an Instant Pot pressure cooker. The same general method applies, the only difference being the amount of liquid you are using. When using a pressure cooker you need about half as much liquid to braise than with the traditional method.

1. Season the short ribs with salt and pepper.

2. Turn the Instant Pot to the sauté setting and add the oil. Once the oil begins to shimmer, place the shorts ribs in and sear them until they have a deep brown crust on all sides, about 7 minutes. If you can't fit all the short ribs in at once sear in separate batches.

3. Transfer the short ribs to a plate and set aside.

4. Add the onions to the pot, stirring them every now and then until golden brown, about 5 minutes.

5. Add the tomato paste and stir until it gives off a sweet aroma, about 1 minute.

6. Add the red wine and stir with a wooden spoon to scrape up and fond on the bottom of the pot.

7. Simmer the wine for about 3 minutes to cook off some of the harshness of the alcohol and to reduce.

8. Add the short ribs back into the pot along with any juices that might have been released when resting.

9. Pour in the beef stock. When using an Instant Pot, the liquid should only cover about ⅓ to ½ of the meat.

10. Place the lid on the Instant Pot and set to high-pressure cook for 45 minutes. Allow pressure to release naturally for 10 minutes then rapid release any of the remaining steam.

11. Remove the short ribs from the pot and bring the liquid up to a simmer to reduce into a sauce.

12. Serve the short ribs warm with roasted vegetables (page 150).

BRAISED SHORT RIB SANDWICH

Braised short ribs

Ciabatta bread

1 yellow onion, sliced into rings

Pinch of salt

3 Tbsp of butter

1 slice of pepper jack cheese

Half a spoonful of mayonnaise

½ tsp of horseradish

Half a spoonful of spicy mustard

Serves 1

1. Braise the short ribs as previously instructed (page 94).

2. Slice the onion into rings. To do so, place the onion on its rounded side and slice straight down lengthwise.

3. Place a pan on medium heat and add 2½ tablespoon of butter.

4. Once the butter is melted and bubbling add the sliced onion and salt.

5. Stir frequently for around 20 minutes until the onion rings reduce significantly in size and get a deep brown color on them. The natural sugars in the onion will begin to caramelize. The onions should be sweet and sticky. (You can deglaze the pan with a swig of red wine vinegar if available, but it is not necessary.)

6. Slice the bread and lightly toast it in a pan with your remaining butter.

7. Combine the horseradish, mayonnaise, and mustard and spread over the buns.

8. Top the bottom bun with short ribs and cheese.

9. Place the sandwich open-faced in the oven with the broiler set to high. (Remember the broiler is a coil in the oven that provides high direct heat, perfect for quickly melting cheese.)

10. Broil until the cheese is bubbling, this will happen fast so keep an eye on it.

11. Once the cheese is melted, top the sandwich with caramelized onions and the remaining bun.

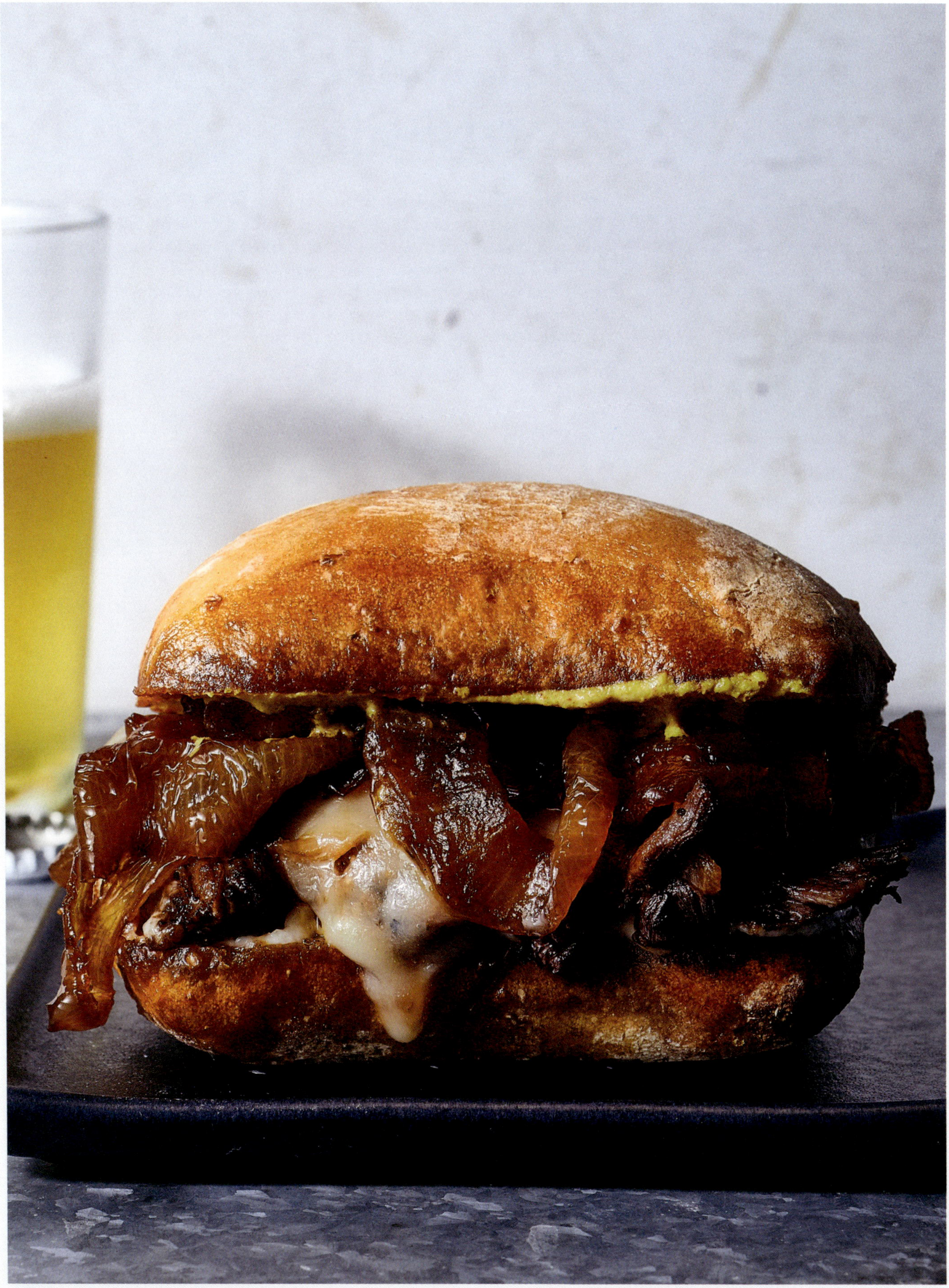

FULLY LOADED BRAISED BEEF NACHOS

One of my favorite things to make with braised beef chuck is fully loaded nachos. They're a perfect snack to eat while watching the big game. I braise the beef in an Instant Pot, but again this can be made in the traditional fashion by using more liquid. You could braise the beef just as you did the short ribs, but since it's for nachos why not add a few more spices to the mix, and swap out the red wine for beer to kick it up a notch.

2 lbs beef chuck roast (pre-packaged chuck cubes work as well but a whole roast is preferable)

1½ tsp of salt

2 Tbsp of brown sugar

2 tsp of chili powder

1½ tsp of cumin

1 tsp of garlic powder

1 yellow onion, thinly sliced

1 Tbsp of vegetable oil

12 oz can beer

For the nachos:

1 bag of corn tortilla chips

1 jalapeño, sliced (I will show you how to quickly pickle it, but store-bought pickled jalapeños can be subbed)

¼ cup white vinegar

½ Tbsp white sugar

½ red onion, diced

1 Roma tomato, diced

2½ cups of pepper jack cheese

Fresh guacamole (page 143)

1 lime, cut into wedges

Serves 6

Tip: If you don't have the required seasonings, simply sub them out for 3 tablespoons of a taco seasoning packet.

1. Combine the seasonings and brown sugar in a bowl then rub the mixture onto the beef chuck, coating it thoroughly.

2. Turn the Instant Pot to the sauté setting and add the oil.

3. Once the oil is shimmering, sear the chuck on all sides. (About 3 minutes a side or until a deep crust has formed.)

4. Add the sliced onions into the pot over the beef and pour in the beer.

5. If using an Instant Pot close lid and switch the vent to sealing. Set to high pressure for 55 minutes.

6. Allow the pressure to release naturally for 10 minutes then manually release the remaining steam.

7. If braising traditionally a second can of beer is required, fill the pot until two-thirds of the beef is covered with liquid.

8. Bring to a simmer and cover, then place in the oven at 325°F for 3½ to 4 hours.

9. Once the chuck has finished braising, shred it into the cooking juices using two forks.

(Continued on next page)

NOT YOUR MOTHER'S COOKBOOK

Assembling the nachos:

1. Set the oven to 375°F.

2. To quickly pickle the jalapeño, thinly slice it and place it in a bowl. Pour the vinegar and sugar over the slices and let the mixture sit for at least 20 minutes. This will not fully pickle them as you'd find in a jar at the store, but the vinegar will begin to break down the cell walls of the jalapeños, taking the edge off while still giving you some bite.

3. Line a baking sheet with tin foil and cover with an even layer of tortilla chips.

4. Cover the chips with cheese and shredded beef. Repeat to create more layers if desired. Top with any remaining cheese.

5. Bake until the cheese is oozing and bubbling, about 7–10 minutes should do the trick.

6. Top with the jalapeños, tomato, onion, and guacamole.

7. Squeeze over fresh lime and serve.

ASIAN FUSION STICKY RIBS

Full rack of pork baby back ribs

Dry rub:

3 Tbsp of brown sugar

1½ Tbsp of chili powder

2 tsp of ginger powder

2 tsp of Chinese five spice (can substitute allspice)

2 tsp of garlic powder

2 tsp of onion powder

1½ tsp of salt

1 tsp Szechuan pepper (If available. If you can't find it, don't worry.)

Cooking liquid:

½ cup of water

½ cup of pineapple juice

¼ cup of apple cider vinegar

A thumb-sized piece of ginger, smashed

2 cloves of garlic, smashed

Sauce:

¼ cup of reserved dry rub

6 Tbsp of hoisin sauce

2 Tbsp of apple cider vinegar

2 Tbsp of soy sauce

2 Tbsp of honey

1 Tbsp of Worcestershire sauce

1 Tbsp of fresh ginger, minced

2 cloves of fresh garlic, minced

¼ cup of ketchup

Serves 2

Ribs can also be made with ease in an Instant Pot. They only take 25 minutes and will fall off the bone like no rib you've had before.

1. Begin by removing the membrane from the back of the ribs. Make a small incision with a knife or scrape the membrane back slightly with a spoon. Using a towel, grip the membrane, and pull it off.
2. Pat the ribs dry and rub them thoroughly with the dry rub mix. Reserve ¼ cup of the rub to use in your sauce.
3. Fill the Instant Pot with the water, vinegar, pineapple juice, ginger, and garlic. Then place the cooking rack of the Instant Pot over the liquid.
4. Place the ribs inside the Instant Pot (you can wrap them around the inside of the pot or cut the rack in half and place them in side by side.)
5. Close the lid and switch the vent to sealing.
6. Set to high pressure and cook for 25 minutes.
7. Remove the ribs and brush generously with the sauce.
8. Broil the ribs on high for 5 minutes or until sauce begins to bubble and char slightly.
9. Garnish with spring onions and sesame seeds.

The sauce:

1. While the ribs are cooking, place a saucepan on medium heat.
2. Add ¼ cup of the reserved dry rub along with minced ginger and garlic to the saucepan.
3. Add the vinegar, soy, worcestershire and stir until the rub is dissolved.
4. Next add the ketchup, honey, hoisin sauce, and stir until combined.
5. Simmer on low for 10–15 minutes.

NOT YOUR MOTHER'S COOKBOOK

BEEF

MELT IN YOUR MOUTH BEEF TACOS

Fuck it, I guess I'm on a bit of an Instant Pot kick, let's finish it off with some braised beef tacos.

1 beef chuck roast (pre-packaged chuck cubes work as well but a whole roast is preferable)

1 yellow onion, diced

2 Tbsp of olive oil

½ cup of beef broth

Juice of 1 lime

2 Tbsp of chili powder

1 Tbsp of cumin

1 Tbsp of chili lime seasoning

½ Tbsp of garlic powder

Pinch of salt & pepper

Queso fresco for garnish

Avocado purée:

2 ripe avocados

Juice of 2 limes

A handful of green onions (about 3–5)

1 jalapeño, cut into pieces

1 clove of garlic

Pinch of salt & pepper

1 bunch of cilantro (save some for garnishing)

Serves 4

Tip: Spices can be subbed out for 3 tablespoons from a taco seasoning packet.

1. Season the beef chuck with salt and pepper.
2. Place the Instant Pot pressure cooker on the sauté setting and pour in the olive oil.
3. Once the pot is hot, sear the chuck on all sides until a crust forms (about 3 minutes a side).
4. Once seared, remove the chuck and add in the diced onion.
5. Add the spices to the diced onions and stir. Sauté for 3 minutes.
6. Pour the beef broth over the onions and squeeze in the juice of one lime.
7. Place the beef chuck on top of the broth and onion mixture.
8. Switch the Instant Pot to the 'meat stew' setting and close the lid. Set thecook time to 45 minutes.
9. While the beef is cooking, combine the ingredients for the purée in a blender and blend until smooth.
10. Heat the tortillas over an open flame or wrap them in tin foil and place them in a 200°F oven for 10 minutes.
11. Once the beef is cooked, allow the Instant Pot to naturally release it's pressure for 10 minutes then manually release the remaining steam.
12. Shred the beef into the juices of the pot with a fork.
13. Scoop out the beef with a slotted spoon or tongs and pile into warm tortillas and top with the avocado purée.
14. Garnish with queso fresco and cilantro.

BEEF

BEER POACHED BRATS

4 Bratwursts & buns
2 cans of beer
2 bell peppers, sliced
1 yellow onion, sliced
1 Tbsp of butter
Pinch of salt & pepper

Serves 4

Poaching is a similar technique to braising, in that you are cooking in a flavored liquid. However, when poaching you are not using a protein with a lot of connective tissue and therefore you do not need to cook it for anywhere near as long. Cooking brats in beer is an example of poaching.

1. Thinly slice the onions and peppers.
2. Place a pot on medium-high heat, and add butter.
3. Once the butter is melted and bubbling add in the sliced onions and peppers.
4. Season with a pinch of salt and pepper.
5. Sauté the onions and peppers for around 3 minutes or until the onions turn slightly brown and the peppers soften.
6. Place the bratwursts on top of onions and peppers and pour over the beer until the brats are fully submerged.
7. Bring the beer to a boil then reduce to simmer for about 12–15 minutes.
8. Remove the brats from the pot and place them on a hot grill or pan to sear for 2 minutes.
9. While the brats are searing, place the pot with the remaining onions, peppers, and beer back on medium-high heat and cook until the beer is reduced completely and you are left with sticky onions and peppers.
10. Take the brats off the grill or remove them from the pan, and place them in the buns.
11. Top with the onions and peppers.

I will close this section on beef by talking about **stews.** A stew is very similar to a braise in the sense that the protein you are stewing requires cooking in moisture to become tender. The difference with stewing is you cover the meat completely with liquid after it has been seared. This liquid becomes the base of your stew and takes on a ton of flavor. You will thicken this liquid just before serving with a roux or a slurry (our two main thickening agents that I discuss in Sauces, page 128).

You often add roughly cut vegetables such as carrots, leeks, and potatoes to stews to make the dish a complete meal in and of itself. Stews are perfect for cold winter days, they are cheap to make, do not require a lot of technical skills, and will leave your home smelling amazing all day.

BASIC BEEF STEW

1 lb of stewing beef (most supermarkets will sell beef chuck cut into cubes, this is known as stewing beef. If you can, buy a chuck roast whole and cut it into cubes yourself.)

3 Tbsp of olive oil

2 cups of beef broth

½ lbs of potatoes, peeled and cut into 2-inch pieces

2 carrots peeled and cut into 1-inch pieces

2 stalks of celery, cut into 1-inch pieces

1 yellow onion, diced

Pinch of salt & pepper

Serves 4

This cheesesteak recipe makes for a killer sandwich with relatively minimal effort. You can splurge and use an expensive cut of beef such as a ribeye, but because you are slicing the meat so thin and cooking it through, a cheaper cut like a flank steak will work just fine.

1. Place a pot on medium-high heat, allow it to heat up (3 minutes) then add the oil.

2. Salt and pepper the stewing meat thoroughly.

3. Sear the meat in the pot, browning on all sides. Be sure to sear each side of the chunk of beef. This should take around 7 minutes.

4. Remove the seared beef from the pot and add the onion, carrots, and celery. Sauté the vegetables for 3 minutes.

5. Once sautéd, deglaze the pot with a splash of red wine, if you don't have wine available, pour in a splash of beef broth.

6. Scrape any bits of fond off the bottom of the pot with a wooden spatula. Then pour in the remaining beef broth to fill the pot.

7. Add the seared beef and its juices back into the pot. If the beef isn't fully submerged add more broth until it is.

8. Add in the potatoes and bring the stew to a boil then reduce the heat to low to simmer.

9. Simmer for 1 to 1½ hours, you'll know the stew is done when the meat is tender and breaks apart with ease.

10. The starch from the potatoes should be enough to thicken the stew, however, if it is not to your desired thickness simply add a slurry and stir. (A slurry is 1 tablespoon of cold water mixed with 1 tablespoon of cornstarch. For more on sluries, see page 128.)

11. Serve the stew in a bowl with a crusty slice of french bread for dipping.

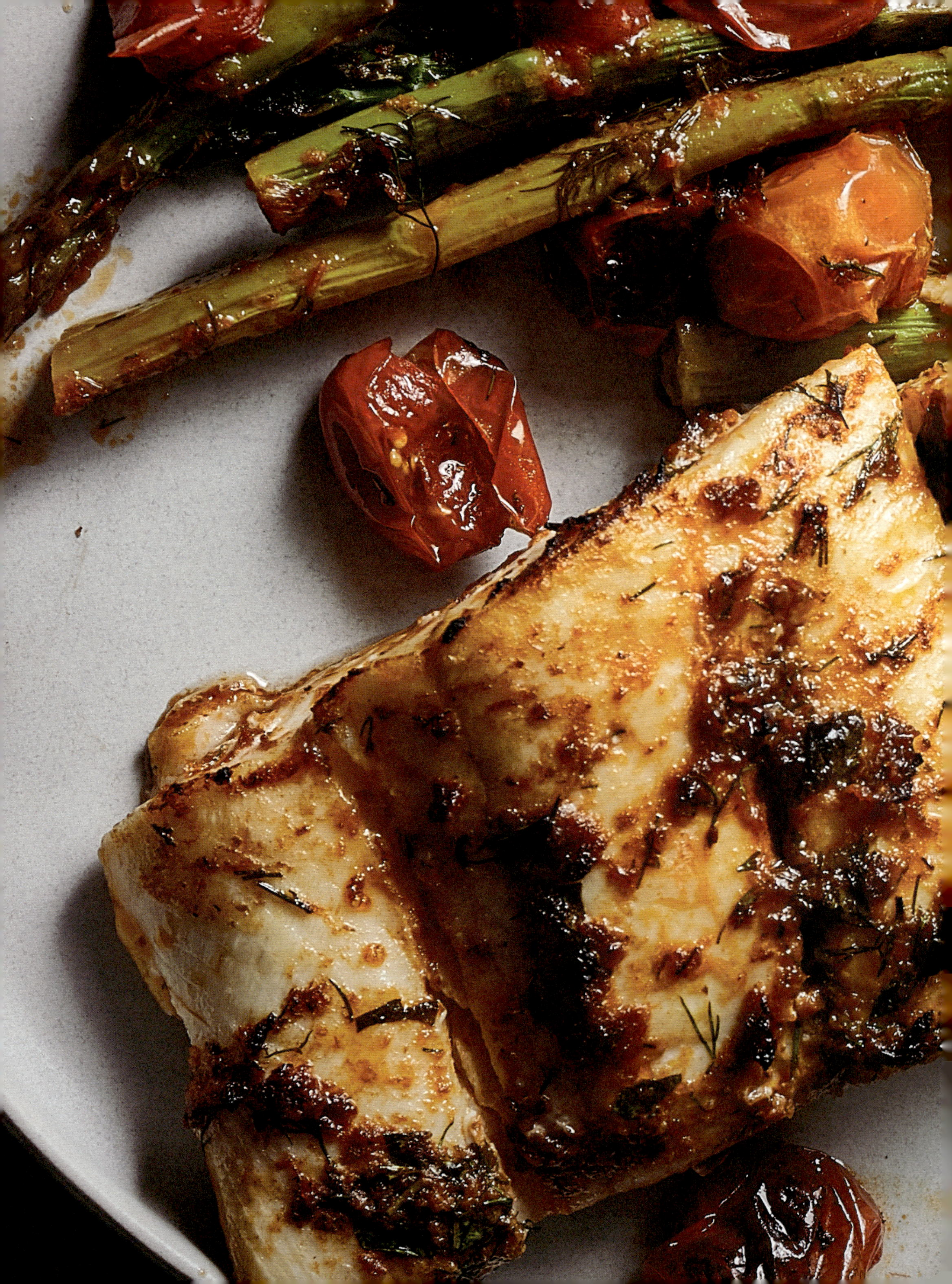

FISH

Alas, you have arrived at fish. In my opinion, fish can be the most difficult protein to cook. It falls apart, it sticks to the pan, some fish only need to be seared while some need to be cooked through. But you've developed some serious cooking skills by this point in the book. You will be using all of those when cooking fish.

When cooking any protein, but especially fish, it is important to have the freshest fillet possible. To determine freshness you will use your sense of smell, sight, and touch.

The biggest misconception people have about fish, and why some people avoid it, is it smells "fishy". However, this should never be the case when cooking fish. If you are preparing a saltwater fish it should smell like the ocean when it is raw.

If a fish has a strong fishy odor do not buy it—that is the first sign that the fish is not fresh.

When you're at the supermarket look at the eyes of the fish they are selling. They should be crystal clear. If they are cloudy or spotty do not buy that fish, it is not fresh.

Finally, fish should have a firm texture to it. If you poke a fillet and it holds the indentation of your finger, it is not fresh. The fillet should spring back to life once your finger is removed.

Once you have determined the fish you are cooking is fresh you can begin.

As in the previous chapters, we will begin by pan searing fish. Generally, fish that you pan sear is meatier, more oily, and richer in flavor. Fish such as swordfish, tuna, halibut, and salmon are great for pan searing. We will begin with the most commonly cooked fish, salmon.

PAN SEARED SALMON

1 Tbsp of olive oil

4 oz salmon fillet

Pinch of salt & pepper

Serves 1

I love nothing more than pan seared salmon with crispy skin. In my opinion, when cooked correctly, the skin is the best part. I have found that people rarely eat the skin of the salmon. Let me tell you—if you don't, you're missing out. Salmon skin has a ton of fat in it, the good fat too, the omega 3s your doctor tells you you need more of. So not only is salmon skin the most nutritious part of the fish, the high-fat content allows it to crisp up wonderfully.

1. First, you must prepare the salmon for the perfect sear. To do this you must remove the scales from the skin. This is a crucial step that often goes overlooked.

2. To remove the scales simply take a knife and scrape back and forth along the skin, the scales should begin to fly off (I recommend doing this over the sink or garbage can because it can get messy).

3. Once the scales are removed pat the fillet dry with a towel (remember that moisture is the enemy of a good sear).

4. Once dry, season with a pinch of salt and pepper. Remember to do this right before searing because the salt will begin to draw the moisture out.

5. Place a pan on medium-high heat. Once it is hot (water jumps out when flicked in) add in the olive oil. The oil should coat the bottom of the pan, depending on the size of your pan you might need more oil. If the pan is at the proper temperature the oil should begin to shimmer.

6. Place the salmon in the pan skin side down, and lightly press down on it to ensure the skin has even contact with the pan. Once the salmon is set do not attempt to move it until the flip.

7. You will cook the salmon the majority of the way through on the skin side. This will be about 6 minutes (time will vary depending on thickness).

8. Notice that the color of the fish changes as it cooks. It will turn from bright orange to an opaque duller colored orange. Once the opaque color has covered ¾ of the fish it is ready to flip.

9. Flip the fish and cook on the opposite side for about 1 minute. (I like to eat salmon cooked to medium, so slightly under fully cooked.)

10. Crack the skin with your fork and dig in.

FISH

NOT YOUR MOTHER'S COOKBOOK

Ahi Tuna Tacos with Avocado Slaw

1 Ahi tuna steak

1 avocado, diced

½ cup of red cabbage, sliced

2 Tbsp of rice wine vinegar (can sub for white vinegar)

½ tsp of soy sauce

½ red onion, thinly sliced

½ cucumber, diced

1 bunch of cilantro, minced

3 green onions, thinly sliced

Juice of ½ a lime

2 Tbsp of salsa verde

⅓ cup of mayonnaise

2 Tbsp of sriracha

6 flour tortillas

Sesame seeds for garnish

Serves 4

1. To make the slaw, mix the cabbage, red onion, green onion, salsa verde, lime juice, cilantro, avocado, soy sauce and vinegar in a large mixing bowl.

2. Set the slaw in the fridge to allow the flavors to blend together.

3. Sear the tuna steak as instructed on page 116.

4. Cut the seared tuna into cubes.

5. Stir the sriracha and mayonnaise together until combined and toss with the tuna in a mixing bowl.

6. Mix until all the pieces of tuna are coated in the sauce.

7. Warm the tortillas over an open flame on the stovetop or wrap them in tin foil and place them in a 200°F oven for 10 minutes.

8. Build the tacos. Start by spooning in the avocado slaw into a tortilla, then top with tuna.

9. Garnish with fresh cilantro, a squeeze of lime, and sesame seeds.

NOT YOUR MOTHER'S COOKBOOK 115

SEARED TUNA STEAK

Ahi tuna steak

1 Tbsp of vegetable oil

Pinch of salt

Serves 1

Ahi tuna. I'm not talking about the shit that comes in a can, I'm talking about that beautiful deep purplish-red ahi tuna steak. This fish requires very little cooking. It's a sushi-grade fish, meaning it can be eaten raw. You want to sear just enough so a light crust forms on the outside but no more. When you slice into a tuna steak the inside should still be that deep purple color.

1. Pat the tuna steak dry and salt each side.

2. Place a pan on medium-high heat, allow the pan to heat up (around 3 minutes) then add the oil. The oil should shimmer in the pan.

3. Lay the tuna steak into the pan.

4. Sear for 1 minute on each side for rare, which is the doneness I recommend. If you are uncomfortable eating it rare then sear for 2 minutes on each side.

5. Let the tuna rest for 5 minutes then slice it into pieces on a 45° angle.

When **pan frying fish** it is important you choose the right kind of fish. You want to avoid fish that are high in oils such as salmon, tuna, swordfish, and trout. These fish are denser and have a texture similar to a steak, as well as a stronger flavor. When fried, these fish tend to dry out on the outside before the inside can be fully cooked. Unlike a chicken breast, you can't pound a fish fillet thin to ensure even frying, the protein is too delicate and will turn mushy and/or fall apart. Fish that fry up well are cod, tilapia, haddock, and catfish.

A general rule to follow to determine whether a fish will fry well is if it is a freshwater fish with white flesh. These fish are more neutral in flavor than the oily fish mentioned previously, which allows you to add flavors in the breading process. When breading fish for pan frying you will follow the same general breading steps you learned previously in the book.

It's important to note that, like chicken, you do not pan fry fish with the skin on. The fish I mentioned above that are good for frying are generally sold with the skin already off. However, you can always ask the butcher to remove it for you if you are buying a whole fish or large fillet. For the purposes of this book, I will not be going into detail about how to break down a whole fish, that is a skill that requires a lot of technique, multiple knives, and a lot of practice, and after all, this is a book for beginners.

PAN FRIED BREADED TILAPIA

1 tilapia fillet

½ cup of flour

¼ cup of vegetable oil for frying

2 eggs, beaten

1 cup of breadcrumbs (I use panko)

2 Tbsp of cajun seasoning or Old Bay

Pinch of salt & pepper

Serves 1

Since tilapia is a neutral-flavored fish, you will spice it up by adding some seasoning to the breading. This is where you can get creative and begin playing with flavor combinations. Add a Cajun seasoning blend to spice it up. Try chili powder, cumin, and lime zest to create a Tex-Mex flavor. Go with parmesan and parsley for a taste of Italy. Although I'm using a tilapia fillet, know this can be done with any of the frying fish previously mentioned.

1. Prepare the breading set up by beating the eggs into a dish, pouring the flour on a plate, and mixing the breadcrumbs with salt, pepper, and Cajun seasoning.

2. Pat the fish dry and dredge in flour. Next place into the beaten eggs, coating each side thoroughly, and finish by rolling in seasoned breadcrumbs.

3. Place a pan on medium-high heat and add the oil, allow the oil to heat up for 10 minutes.

4. Check the oil temperature by flicking in some spare breadcrumbs. They should begin to bubble right away and turn golden brown.

5. Gently lay fish in the oil, remembering to lay away from your body to avoid being burned by jumping oil.

6. Fry on each side for about 3 minutes. As with anything you pan fry you are looking at the color of the bread crumbs to determine when the fish is done. You can't poke at the protein as you would do when searing other proteins, so you must use visual cues to determine doneness.

PAN FRIED TILAPIA SANDWICH WITH FRESH SLAW

1 pan fried tilapia fillet

¼ cup of red cabbage, sliced

1 green onion, thinly sliced

½ of a cucumber, thinly sliced

3 Tbsp white vinegar

½ tsp of sugar

¼ cup of mayonnaise

½ tsp cajun seasoning mix or Old Bay

1 brioche bun

½ Tbsp of butter for toasting the bun

Serves 1

1. Pan fry the tilapia as instructed in the previous recipe (page 118).
2. Mix the sliced cabbage, green onion, cucumber, sugar, and vinegar in a bowl. Set aside.
3. Mix the cajun seasoning or Old Bay with mayonnaise.
4. Add the butter to a pan on medium-low heat and toast the bun until golden.
5. Spread the seasoned mayonnaise on both slices of the bun.
6. Remove the slaw from the bowl, squeezing gently to strain off any excess vinegar, and place on the bottom of the bun. Top with the fried tilapia fillet and top bun.

Alright, I've covered a lot of pan frying so far in this book. Let's now introduce a new method of breading known as **battering.** Unlike traditional breading, when you batter a protein you coat it in a thick wet mixture of flour, seasonings, and a liquid (sometimes eggs). It is similar to the consistency of a pancake batter. This creates a light and crispy coating on your protein. Battered foods are typically deep-fried in a pot of oil. However, you can achieve the same result when pan frying by flipping the battered protein halfway through cooking and using slightly more oil, about ¾ of an inch in the pan. In order to accommodate for the extra oil, you will need to use a pan that has a higher rim—a cast iron pan works well.

BEER BATTERED CODFISH

1 lb cod fillet, cut into 4 equal portions

1 cup of all-purpose flour

1 tsp of Old Bay Seasoning

1 tsp of salt

1 tsp of pepper

12 oz can of beer

1 egg, beaten

Vegetable oil for frying (you'll need enough to fill your pan up with ¾ of an inch of oil)

Squeeze of fresh lemon to finish

Serves 4

I think the best way to batter fish is with a beer batter. Ever had fish n' chips at a restaurant? That's exactly what we're going for. Codfish works extremely well when beer battered, but again you can use any of the neutral-flavored fish as we discussed previously for this dish.

1. Heat the oil on medium-high heat until it reaches 350°F, about 10 minutes on the stove will achieve this.

2. In a large bowl whisk together the flour, Old Bay Seasoning, salt and pepper, and the beaten egg.

3. Slowly pour in the beer, mixing with a whisk as you go to ensure there are no lumps in the batter. Whisk until smooth.

4. Pat the fillets of cod dry with a towel then season with a pinch of salt and pepper.

5. Fully submerge the cod fillet in the batter, ensuring the entire fish is coated. (It's okay if you can see the fish through the batter when you pull it out.)

6. Gently lay the battered fish into the oil, it should begin to bubble immediately.

7. Cook for 3–4 minutes or until golden then flip and cook for an additional 3–4 minutes.

8. Remove from the pan and place on a paper towel to drain off any excess oil.

9. Serve with a squeeze of fresh lemon.

BROILED MISO GLAZED SALMON

6 oz salmon fillet

1 Tbsp of miso paste (this is a fermented soybean paste. It can be found in the world foods section of the grocery store)

2 Tbsp of brown sugar

2 Tbsp of soy sauce

¼ cup of carrots, shredded

¼ cup of broccoli florets (the tips of the broccoli)

1 Tbsp of olive oil

1 clove of garlic, minced

½ Tbsp of ginger, minced

Serves 1

Remember that broiling is a method of cooking using high direct heat. Like pan searing, this is a very quick way of cooking the fish. This method allows you to glaze the fish with a sticky sauce, creating a delicious layer of flavor on the flesh of your fish. The trade-off with this method is you will not have the crispy skin, but if you do not care for eating the skin then this is a great method for you. As you'll notice in this recipe you are using sugar, and sugar burns at high heats. This is why you line the baking sheet with tin foil. The runoff from the glaze may burn on the tinfoil, and it is much easier to simply throw that foil away than to have to clean the glaze directly off the pan. The moisture from the salmon prevents the glaze from burning on the surface of the fish.

1. Set the broiler on the oven to high.

2. In a bowl mix together the miso paste, sugar, and soy sauce until the sugar is dissolved and the mixture is smooth.

3. Pour the mixture over your salmon fillet making sure the fillet is coated evenly.

4. Place the salmon on a sheet tray with tin foil.

5. Broil the salmon on high for 10–13 minutes.

6. While the fish is broiling, sautée the carrots and broccoli in a pan with olive oil.

7. After about 4 minutes add in the fresh ginger and garlic, and cook for an additional 2 minutes.

8. Serve the salmon on top of the sautéed vegetables.

NOT YOUR MOTHER'S COOKBOOK

FISH

ROASTED HALIBUT WITH CHERRY TOMATOES & ASPARAGUS

12 oz halibut fillet, cut into 2 pieces

Juice of 1 lemon

½ cup of olive oil

3 Tbsp of sundried tomato paste (this can be found in the jarred foods section of the store)

3 cloves of garlic, minced

1 Tbsp of fresh dill, minced

A handful of fresh basil, minced

½ lb of cherry tomatoes

⅓ lb of asparagus

Pinch of salt & pepper

Serves 4

Let's discuss roasting and broiling fish. In my opinion, these are the easiest ways to cook fish. It does not require much technical skill and it makes cooking for a larger group of people much easier.

1. Preheat the oven to 425°F.

2. Combine the olive oil, lemon juice, sun-dried tomatoes, garlic, dill, basil, salt, and pepper in a mixing bowl.

3. Lay the tomatoes and asparagus on a sheet tray and pour a few tablespoons of the oil mixture you just made over them.

4. Toss the vegetables around in the pan until they are all evenly coated then push them to one side of the tray making sure they are spread out in one even layer. Do not stack any of the vegetables on top of each other, this will cause them to steam rather than roast.

5. Place the halibut fillets in the bowl with the remaining oil mixture, and flip them around until all the pieces are evenly coated.

6. Place the halibut on the empty side of the tray and pour over any of the remaining oil mixture.

7. Place the tray in the oven and roast for around 10 minutes.

8. After 10 minutes transfer the tray to the top rack of the oven and turn your broiler on high.

9. Broil for 5 minutes. This will create a bit of a char on the fish as well as on the vegetables.

10. Remove the tray from the oven. You'll know the halibut is cooked properly if it flakes apart with ease.

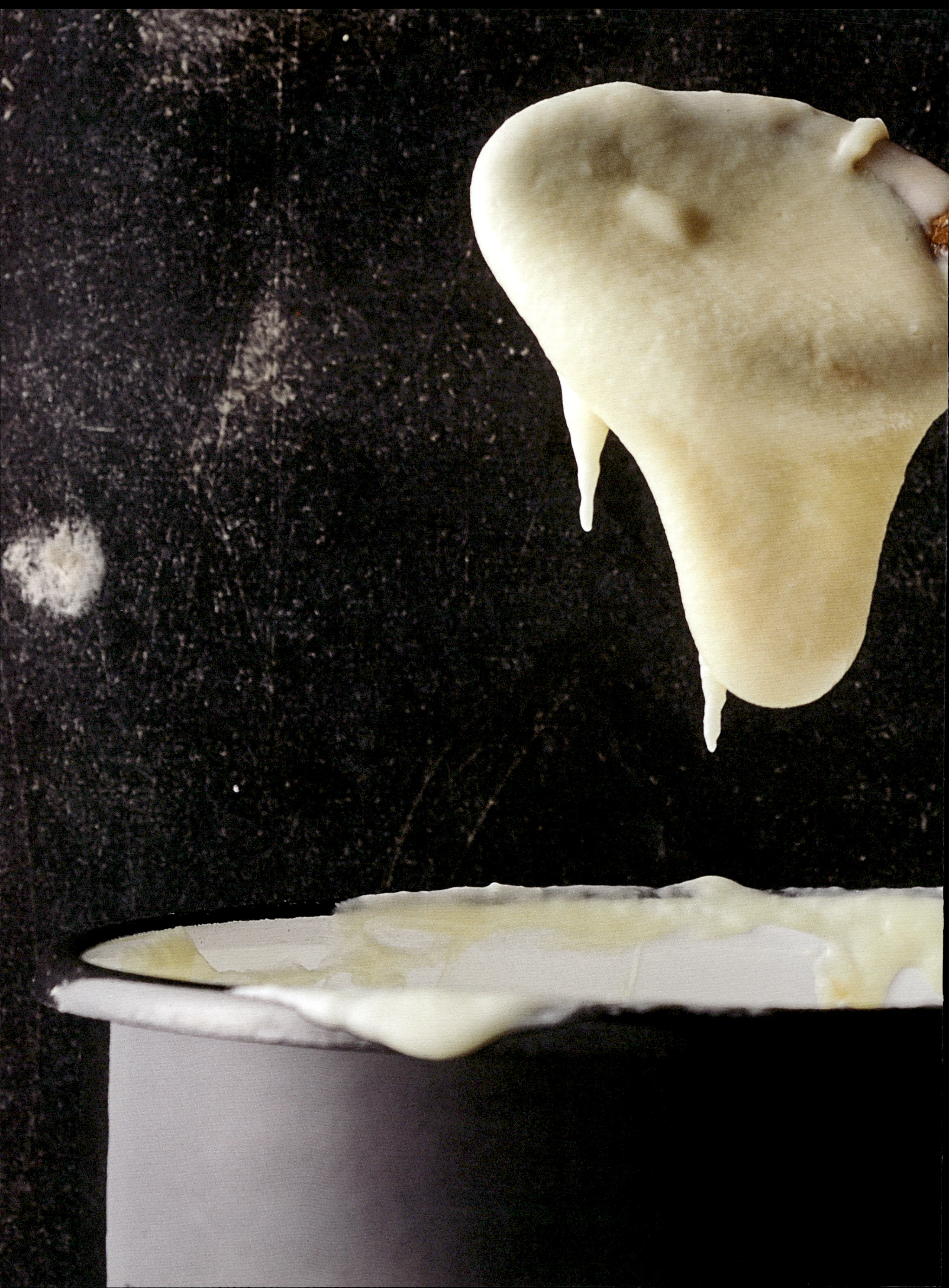

SAUCES

The ability to make sauces is another skill that is often overlooked when it comes to home cooking. The reality is, most, if not all of the sauces I am about to teach you to make can be purchased pre-made in a grocery store. It may seem easier to just grab a jar of tomato sauce off the shelf and call it a day, but the truth is the basic sauces aren't hard to make and they will make your dishes taste exponentially better. Are some sauces hard to make? Absolutely. I won't cover those in this book. I will stick to basic sauces that even the least experienced cook will be able to recreate.

There are two main ways to thicken a sauce. You can make a roux or a slurry. A roux is an equal mixture of flour and fat, most of the time butter, that is cooked together in a saucepan over medium heat. A slurry is a combination of equal parts cold water and cornstarch. A slurry is added to a sauce at the end of the cooking process whereas a roux is made at the beginning and becomes the base for your sauce.

You can make different kinds of rouxs depending on how long you cook them. A roux can go from white/blonde to brown/black in color. A white roux is cooked for less time and tends to taste more like the fat you mixed it with. A darker roux is cooked longer and has a much deeper caramelized flavor. For the purposes of this book, you will only be using white/blonde rouxs. The basic formula for a roux is to mix 2 tablespoons of fat with 2 tablespoons of flour combined with one cup of liquid.

Let's use a roux to make a classic béchamel sauce (otherwise known as white sauce). This is one of the five French mother sauces and is the base for dishes such as casseroles, soufflés, and cheese sauces. You will be using it in this book to make homemade Mac N' Cheese. The four other French mother sauces consist of tomato, velouté, espagnole, and hollandaise. In this book I will only be covering béchamel and tomato, for they are the two easiest.

BÉCHAMEL

2 Tbsp of butter

2 Tbsp of flour

1 cup warm milk

Pinch of salt & pepper

Once you learn how to make a basic white sauce, we can build on that to make some homemade mac 'n' cheese (page 130).

1. Place a saucepan on medium heat and add the butter.

2. Once the butter is melted add the flour and stir rapidly with a whisk. The mixture will be wet and thin at first, this is okay.

3. Continue stirring for around 5 minutes to cook some of the harshness of the flour flavor out.

4. The roux should begin to turn a golden blonde color.

5. Begin by adding 1–2 tablespoons of milk to the roux and stir with a whisk. At first, the roux will be clumpy and it may break apart into chunks in the milk, this is okay. Keep stirring and slowly adding milk until the roux loosens back up and turns smooth.

6. Pour in the remaining milk and whisk until smooth.

7. Continue whisking until you are left with a thick white sauce.

8. Add a pinch of salt and pepper to complete the dish.

NOT YOUR MOTHER'S COOKBOOK

BACON & ROSEMARY MAC 'N' CHEESE

8 oz box of macaroni noodles

3 slices of bacon, diced

1 sprig of fresh rosemary, finely chopped

2 Tbsp of butter

2 Tbsp of flour

1 cup of whole milk

1 cup of cheddar cheese, grated

1 cup of smoked gouda cheese, grated

Pinch of salt & pepper

Serves 2

This is a great dish to make in the cold winter months when you need something to warm the soul and stick to your insides. You can omit the bacon and rosemary and still have a wonderful mac 'n' cheese.

1. Begin by rendering the diced bacon in a frying pan. To do so add the diced bacon to a cold pan and place it on medium heat. Stir the bacon frequently until the fat has melted away.

2. Cook the macaroni in salted water according to the box instructions.

3. While the bacon is rendering and pasta is cooking, prepare your white sauce as instructed previously (page 129).

4. Once the white sauce is complete, slowly add in the cheese while stirring.

5. Stir until the cheese is melted then add a pinch of salt and pepper.

6. Add the fresh chopped rosemary to the bacon pan and stir for 1 minute.

7. Remove the pan from the heat and, using a slotted spoon, scoop the bacon bits with rosemary onto a paper towel to drain.

8. Strain the pasta and return it to the pot.

9. Pour the cheese sauce over pasta and mix until the noodles are thoroughly coated. Add in some of the bacon and rosemary bits and stir some more.

10. Serve in a bowl with more bits of rosemary and bacon as a garnish.

NOT YOUR MOTHER'S COOKBOOK 131

ALFREDO SAUCE

An Alfredo sauce is a very easy sauce to make. It requires no roux and takes about 10 minutes in total to complete. It is a perfect sauce to whip up when making pasta.

⅓ cup of butter

1 cup of heavy cream

1½ cups of parmesan cheese, grated

1 clove of garlic, minced

Pinch of salt & pepper

Yields 1½ cups

1. Place a saucepan on medium heat and melt the butter. Once melted pour in the heavy cream and whisk together.
2. Bring the mixture to a simmer and cook for 3 minutes.
3. Add the garlic, parmesan, salt and pepper.
4. Stir until the cheese is melted.
5. Serve immediately.

TOMATO SAUCE

A fresh tomato sauce is incredibly easy to make and can be built on to make pizza sauce, vodka sauce, lasagnas, chicken and eggplant parmesans, and much more.

1 Tbsp of olive oil

1 yellow onion, diced

2 cloves of garlic, minced

12 oz can of tomatoes (can be diced, crushed or whole peeled)

A few basil leaves, minced

Pinch of chili flake

Pinch of salt & pepper

Yields 12 oz

1. Place a pan on medium heat and add the olive oil.
2. Sweat the onions with a pinch of salt, and chili flake for 2 minutes, or until they become translucent. (Sweating onions is different from sautéing them. When you sauté you use a higher heat and brown the onions, which in turn makes them sweeter. For this sauce you do not want that sweetness so you will sweat them by placing a lid on your pan and cooking the onions until they become translucent.)
3. Once the onions are translucent, add the garlic and stir until aromatic, about 45 seconds to a minute.
4. Pour in the tomatoes and simmer for at least 30 minutes.
5. Add in the basil and simmer for 2-3 minutes.
6. Salt to taste. Blend if desired.

SPICY NOODLES IN PEANUT BUTTER SAUCE

6 Tbsp of peanut butter

2 Tbsp of soy sauce

1 Tbsp of rice wine vinegar

1 tsp of chili oil

2 tsp of sesame oil

1 Tbsp of ginger, finely minced or grated

1 clove of garlic, finely minced or grated

1 fresh red or Thai chili pepper, sliced (you can sub in dried chili flakes if needed)

2 green onions, sliced on a bias

1 packet of udon noodle (can be found in the Asian section of the supermarket)

Serves 2

1. Finely grate the ginger and garlic, and thinly slice the chili.

2. Place a saucepan on medium heat and add the peanut butter, soy sauce, vinegar, oil, garlic, and ginger.

3. Heat the mixture until the peanut butter becomes loose and a sauce forms. (If the peanut butter clumps up, gradually add warm water and stir until the sauce loosens.)

4. Cook the udon noodles according to package instructions.

5. Combine the peanut butter sauce with the udon noodles and stir.

6. Top the noodles with sliced green onions.

If you can remember back to middle school science class you learned that an emulsion happens when two substances that don't usually mix are forced together. You use **emulsification** very often when making sauces. A vinaigrette salad dressing is an example of an emulsion sauce. Normally oil and vinegar don't mix, but when you whisk them together with enough force the oil disperses into tiny particles and becomes suspended in the vinegar. This is known as a temporary emulsion; after some time, the oil and vinegar will separate. However, you can make the emulsion stable and keep the oil in suspension by adding in emulsifiers. Common emulsifiers are egg yolks and mustard. When these are introduced you get a thicker emulsified sauce.

One of my favorite things to do is to make pasta sauces simply by emulsifying the starchy water you cooked the pasta in with olive oil. The starch in the pasta water acts as the emulsifier creating an emulsion between water and oil. Here's an example of that technique; once you understand how it works, you can create all kinds of delicious pasta dishes.

SAUTÉED GARLIC & BROCCOLI RABE PASTA

8 oz spaghetti noodles

5 Tbsp of olive oil

3 cloves of garlic, finely minced

4 pieces of broccoli rabe, sliced into bite-sized pieces.

⅓ cup of fresh parmesan cheese, grated

Squeeze of fresh lemon juice

Pinch of salt & pepper

Serves 2

1. Cook the pasta according to box instructions, being sure to salt the boiling water before putting in the noodles.

2. Place a large sauté pan on medium-high heat and add 4 tablespoons of olive oil, sauté the broccoli rabe for 5 minutes. They should have a nice brown crisp on them.

3. Add the minced garlic and sauté for an additional minute.

4. Strain the pasta but be sure to reserve at least a cup of the pasta water before doing so.

5. Put the pasta back into the pot you cooked it in and add ¼ cup of the pasta water.

6. Now pour in the sautéed broccoli and garlic as well as any residual oil in the pan to the pasta.

7. Begin to swirl the pasta vigorously in the pot. A creamy sauce will begin to form—this is an emulsification of the starchy pasta water and the oil. If a sauce is not forming add another tablespoon or 2 of olive oil. If the sauce is too thick, thin it out with more pasta water. Do so until you have a balanced sauce.

8. Finish by stirring in the cheese and squeezing over some fresh lemon juice.

PANTRY CARBONARA

8 oz of spaghetti or linguine noodles

1 egg

⅓ cup of parmesan cheese, grated

2 slices of bacon, diced

Serves 2

While there's a traditional way to make pasta carbonara, I make a very similar dish using slightly different ingredients. I call it a 'pantry carbonara' because everything needed to make it can usually be found lying around your kitchen, which makes this recipe great for an impromptu meal.

1. Add the diced bacon to a cold pan then place it on medium high heat (the gradual heating of the pan will begin to slowly render out the fat of the bacon).

2. Give the bacon a 5 minute head start before starting to cook the pasta.

3. Bring water to a boil, salt it thoroughly, then drop in the pasta. Cook according to the box instructions.

4. Grate ⅓ cup of parmesan cheese into a bowl with an egg. Beat together the egg and cheese until combined.

5. Once the pasta is done cooking the bacon should be crispy. Leave all the rendered out bacon fat in the pan, this will be your fat for the emulsion.

6. Strain the pasta but be sure to reserve at least a cup of the pasta water before doing so.

7. Ensure the stove is off. Then transfer the pasta back into the pot you cooked it in and pour in the bacon bits with all the rendered out fat.

8. Ladle in around ¼–½ cup of pasta water to the pot and pour in the egg and cheese mixture.

9. Stir vigorously to emulsify the pasta water with the bacon fat and the egg.

NOT YOUR MOTHER'S COOKBOOK

As I mentioned, **salad dressings** are an emulsion sauce. I feel that everyone should make their own salad dressing. They are easy to make, taste better than anything store-bought, and are much healthier for you. The basic ratio for making any kind of salad dressing is to mix 3 parts oil to 1 part acid. So for every 3 tablespoons of oil you would add one tablespoon of acid. Acids are anything that make your lips pucker. Vinegars and lemon juice are the most commonly used acids in salad dressing.

BALSAMIC VINAIGRETTE

1 Tbsp of balsamic vinegar

3 Tbsp of olive oil

Pinch of salt & pepper

Yields ¼ cup

Dressings are also a great area to get creative with flavor combinations. Swap out balsamic vinegar for apple cider vinegar. Add a clove of minced garlic and some Dijon mustard and see what happens.

1. Combine all the ingredients into a mixing bowl and whisk vigorously until emulsified.

FRENCH DRESSING

1 clove of garlic, finely minced

1 Tbsp of apple cider vinegar

3 Tbsp of olive oil

2 tsp of Dijon mustard

Pinch of salt & pepper

Yields ¼ cup

1. Combine all the ingredients in a mixing bowl and whisk vigorously until smooth and emulsified.

Some dressing such as ranch and caesar don't require an emulsification of oil and acid. These dressings are **mayonnaise-based dressings.** Mayonnaise is an emulsification in its own right. You can use store-bought mayonnaise to make the following dressings, or you can make mayonnaise yourself simply by emulsifying an egg with oil and a splash of acid. In this case, you would not want to use olive oil. The flavor of olive oil is a little too strong for mayonnaise. Use a neutral-flavored seed oil like sunflower or grapeseed. When making mayonnaise you must be constantly stirring as you add the oil to the egg. You must also add the oil very slowly so it can properly bind with the egg yolk. If done properly, 1 egg will be able to suspend a full cup of oil.

Mayonnaise can be made in a blender or food processor to take the manual labor out of the process.

MAYONNAISE

1 egg

½ Tbsp of Dijon mustard

1 Tbsp of white wine vinegar

1 cup neutral-flavored oil (I use grapeseed)

Pinch of salt

Yields 1 cup

1. In a mixing bowl whisk together the egg, mustard, vinegar, and salt.

2. While continuously whisking, begin to add in the oil drop by drop. (By drop I mean about 1 teaspoon). Once that drop of oil disappears into the egg and becomes fully incorporated add another drop. Continue doing this until ¼ of the oil has been added.

3. The mixture should be thick, at this point you can be less deliberate with the amount of oil you are adding and can pour the remaining oil in as a slow steady stream. Don't dump it in all at once, let it drizzle in.

4. Once all the oil is added you'll have mayonnaise.

5. Salt it to taste.

6. This fresh mayo will keep for up to a week in your refrigerator.

RANCH DRESSING

½ cup of yogurt

¼ cup mayonnaise (store-bought or homemade)

2 Tbsp of chives, minced

¼ cup of dill, minced

3 cloves of garlic, minced

2 tsp of onion powder

1 tsp of garlic powder

1 tsp of black pepper

Squeeze of fresh lemon juice

Pinch of salt

Yields 1 cup

1. Combine all the ingredients in a mixing bowl and whisk until evenly combined.

CAESAR DRESSING

1 cup of mayonnaise (store-bought or homemade)

1 clove of garlic, minced

The juice from half a lemon (about 1–2 Tbsp)

2 tsp of Dijon mustard

1 tsp of Worcestershire sauce

⅓ cup of fresh parmesan, grated

2 anchovy fillets finely chopped or 1½ tsp of anchovy paste (optional)

Pinch of salt & pepper

Yields 1 cup

1. Combine all the ingredients in a mixing bowl and whisk until evenly combined.

Tip: You can find anchovies where you'd find canned tuna at the grocery store. You do not have to use them but it is traditionally how a caesar dressing is made. I recommend using them, your dressing will not taste 'fishy' when using the amount suggested, rather it will add a depth of umami flavor.

PICO DE GALLO SALSA

2 Roma tomatoes, diced

½ red onion, diced

1 jalapeño pepper, seeded and diced

Juice of 1 lime

½ cup of cilantro, finely chopped

Pinch of salt & pepper

Yields 1 cup

This salsa can be blended to create a smooth style salsa. I love to char up peaches on the grill and mix those in. Charred pineapple works beautifully as well. If you don't have a grill, don't worry. You can char them right in a pan.

1. Dice the tomatoes, onion, and jalapeño. Be sure to remove the seeds and the white part from inside the jalapeño. This is the spiciest part of the pepper and it can overpower the salsa if left in. (If you like a lot of heat, by all means leave the seeds and pith in.)

2. In a mixing bowl combine the diced tomato, onion and jalapeño with the lime juice, cilantro, salt and pepper.

3. If the salsa is too spicy add 1 teaspoon of sugar to counteract the heat. The flavor of the salsa will get more intense as it sits.

GUACAMOLE

2 ripe avocados, smashed

1 jalapeño, seeded and finely diced

½ a red onion, diced

1 bunch of cilantro, finely chopped

Juice of 1 lime

Pinch of salt & pepper

Yields 1½ cups

1. Slice the avocados in half and remove the pit. Scoop the avocados into a bowl and smash them down with a fork.

2. Slice the jalapeño in half lengthwise, remove the seeds and the white pith then finely dice and add to the bowl.

3. Finely dice half a red onion and add that to the mixing bowl with the jalapeño and avocado.

4. Add in the lime juice, cilantro, salt and pepper.

5. Stir until combined. Continue to salt to taste.

NOT YOUR MOTHER'S COOKBOOK

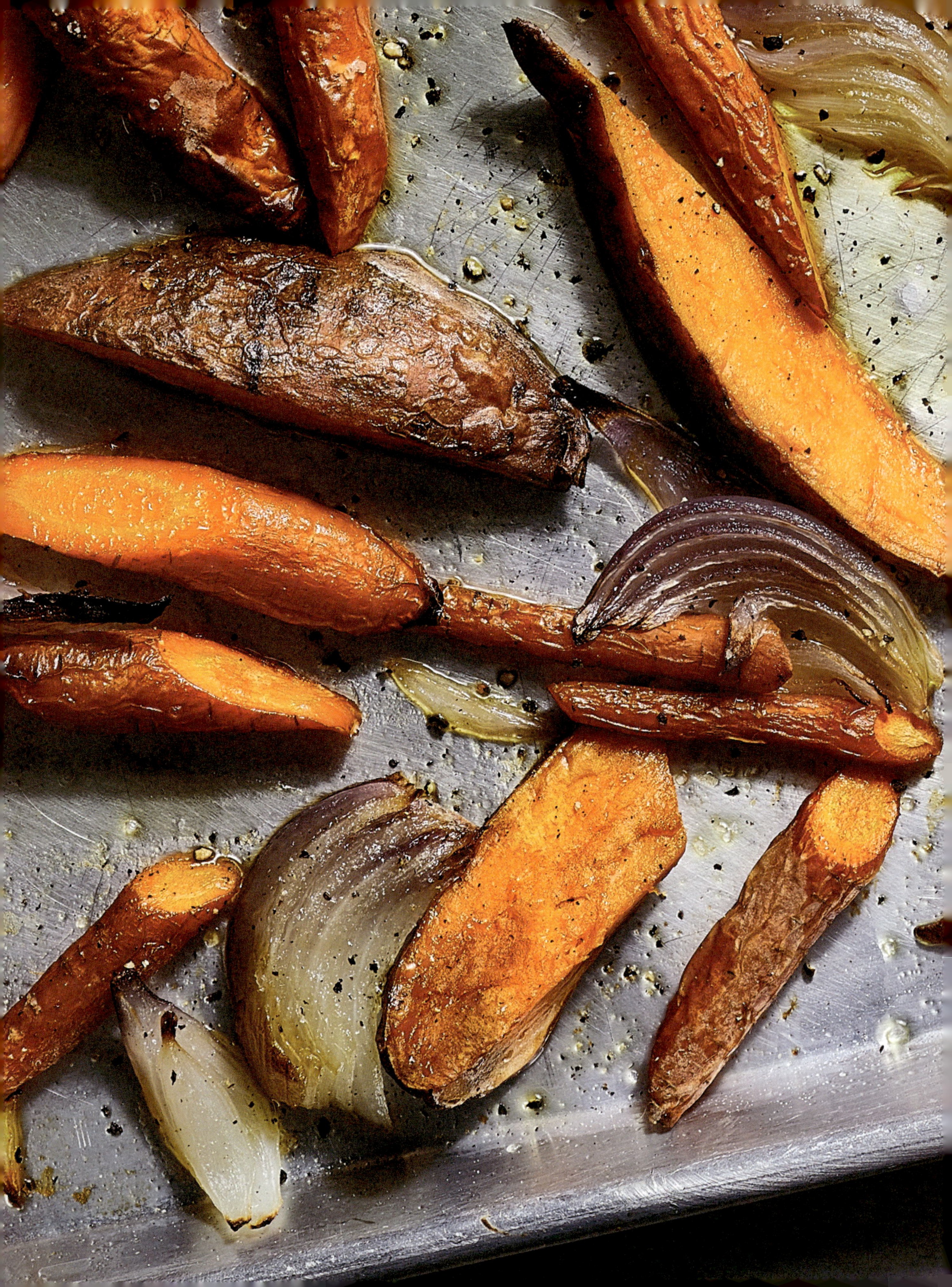

ROASTED VEGETABLES

Roasted vegetables make for a wonderful side to any main dish. There are several things to consider when roasting vegetables. First of all, you need to separate your vegetables based on what category they fall into. Root vegetables such as potatoes, carrots, onions, garlic, and sweet potatoes should be roasted separately from brassicas such as broccoli, brussels sprouts, cauliflower, kale, and cabbage. You separate them in these distinctions because root vegetables will take almost twice the time as brassicas to properly roast. Perfectly roasted brassicas will be light and crispy whereas perfectly roasted root vegetables, due to their high starch and natural sugar content, will be sweet and sticky. Either way, you're in store for a healthy pile of delicious roasted vegetables.

Things to keep in mind:

Don't crowd the pan. Never stack vegetables on top of each other when roasting, as this will cause the vegetables to steam and not roast. You'll be left with mushy vegetables with none of the beautiful roasting color or flavor.

Use a shallow roasting tray. A shallow tray allows for the steam to properly escape and spill over the edge, allowing your vegetables to roast perfectly.

Use plenty of salt and olive oil. The salt will penetrate the vegetables as they roast, bringing out all the flavor. Olive oil will help transfer heat from the pan to the vegetables. It's important that every vegetable is coated with olive oil and has good contact with the pan—meaning that if you slice a brussels sprout in half, put the flat side down on the pan so that the surface will get nice and roasted.

Use proper oven temperature. Mistakes with roasting often happen when the oven temperature is not high enough. When you try to roast at too low of a temperature you'll elongate the cooking process, which will in turn dry out your vegetables without roasting them. 425°F is what I recommend for roasting. Brassicas will take about 25 minutes and root vegetables will take around 45.

ROASTED VEGETABLES

ROASTED BRUSSELS SPROUTS WITH STICKY BALSAMIC REDUCTION

1½ lbs brussels sprouts
3 Tbsp of olive oil
3 Tbsp balsamic vinegar
1 Tbsp of honey
Pinch of salt

Serves 4

1. Preheat the oven to 425°F.

2. Begin by preparing the brussels sprouts for roasting. Trim the woody ends off of the brussels sprouts then slice them in half lengthwise.

3. Layout the brussels sprouts across your pan, making sure they have plenty of space.

4. Drizzle with olive oil and move the brussels sprouts around to ensure they are evenly coated with oil.

5. Salt the brussels sprouts thoroughly.

6. Place the tray in the oven and roast at 425°F for 25 minutes.

7. While the brussels sprouts are roasting, prepare the balsamic reduction.

8. Place a saucepan on medium-heat and add the vinegar and honey.

9. Bring the mixture to a boil then reduce to a simmer and allow the liquid to reduce by half. You'll know it's ready when you dip a spoon in and the reduction holds to the back of the spoon.

10. When the brussels sprouts are done, drizzle the reduction over top, toss and serve warm.

ROASTED VEGETABLES

ROASTED SWEET POTATO WEDGES

3 sweet potatoes

1 tsp of paprika

2 Tbsp of olive oil

Pinch of salt

Serves 4

1. Preheat the oven to 425°F.

2. Rinse the sweet potatoes, being sure to scrub off any dirt.

3. Slice the potatoes into wedge shapes, leaving the skins on.

4. Place the sweet potatoes on a sheet tray and coat with olive oil, salt, and paprika.

5. Shake the pan to evenly coat the potatoes then align them so they each have space to roast.

6. Roast at 425°F for 45 minutes.

BREADED ROASTED ASPARAGUS

1 bunch of asparagus

1 cup of panko breadcrumbs

⅓ cup of fresh parmesan, grated

1 egg, beaten

1 Tbsp of olive oil

Pinch of salt

Serves 4

1. Preheat the oven to 425°F.
2. Rinse the asparagus and cut off the bottom inch of the stalks.
3. Beat 1 egg into a dish. Roll the asparagus in the beaten egg then roll in panko bread crumbs.
4. Place the asparagus on a baking sheet that has been rubbed with olive oil and shred fresh parmesan cheese on top.
5. Roast at 425°F for 20 minutes.

HASSELBACK ROASTED POTATO

1 baking potato

½ stick of butter

A few sprigs of fresh thyme

1 clove of garlic, peeled and smashed

Pinch of salt & pepper

Serves 4

This is a textured potato that will look like an accordion once roasted. You'll have crispy edges and a soft, buttery inside. It's a fantastic way to spice up a boring old roasted potato.

1. Preheat the oven to 425°F.

2. Place 2 chopsticks or wooden spoons on either side of the potato lengthwise. This will prevent your knife from penetrating all the way through the potato when slicing.

3. Slice the potato down to the chopsticks every 1-centimeter to create the hasselback design.

4. Melt the butter in a saucepan with thyme and garlic to infuse the flavors.

5. Generously coat the potato with butter, being sure to brush butter into all the slices you made.

6. Finish with a pinch of salt and pepper.

7. Roast at 425°F for 45 min.

GUEST FEATURES

Here are some fun recipes from other people around the Barstool office. They range in difficulty from 'so easy a child could do it' to slightly more difficult than what I taught you previously in this book. Notice how the methods you learned earlier translate over to a wide variety of recipes.

It should be noted that I have no idea if any of these recipes work.

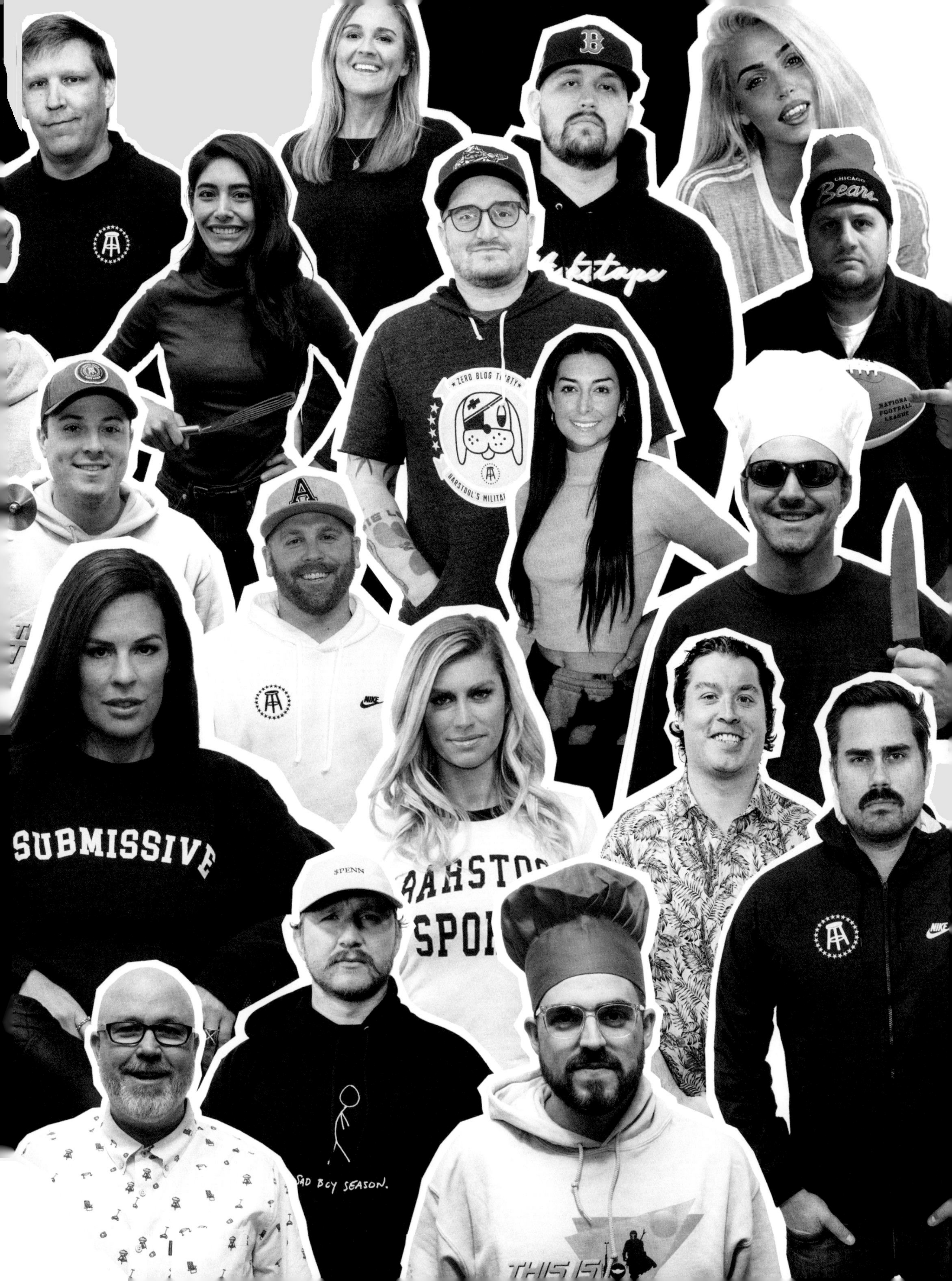
CHICAGO
Bears
SUBMISSIVE
NIKE
$PENN
NIKE
SAD BOY SEASON.

CILANTRO LIME RICE

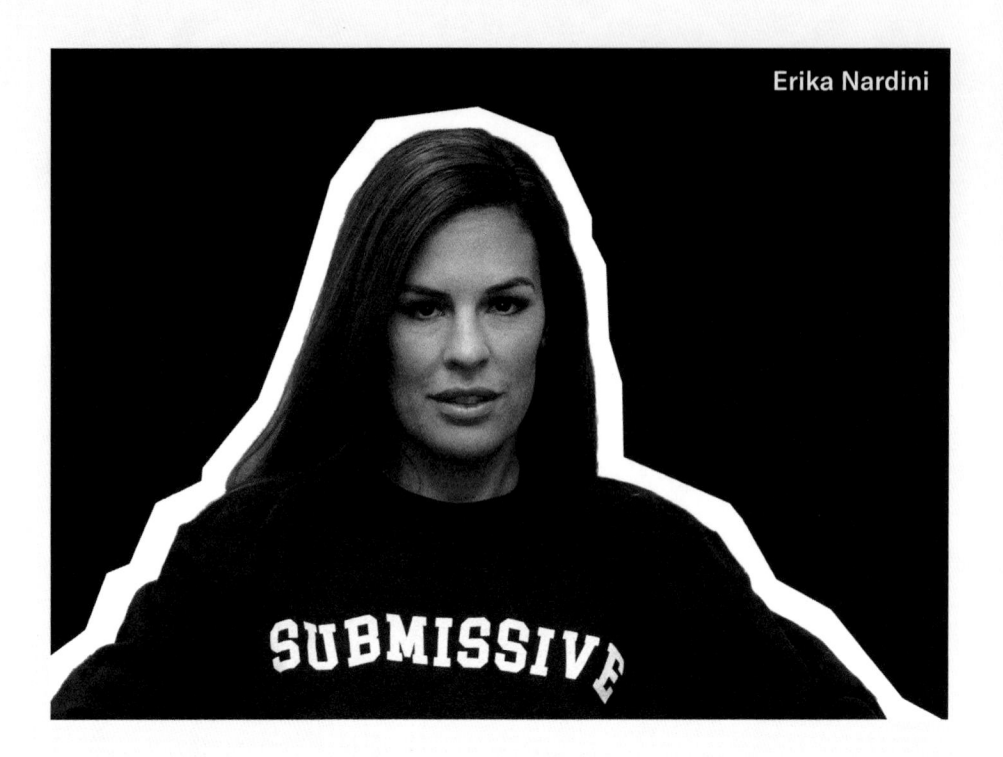

Erika Nardini

1 cup long-grain jasmine rice, rinsed well and drained

1½ cups water

3 tsp extra-virgin olive oil, divided

1 small garlic clove, finely minced

2 scallions, finely chopped

1 Tbsp lime zest

¼ to ½ tsp sea salt

1½ Tbsp lime juice

½ cup finely chopped cilantro

Pinch of red pepper flakes or ¼ diced jalapeño, optional

1. Start by cooking your rice on the stove or in a rice cooker (stovetop instructions are listed in the recipe below). Long-grain white jasmine or basmati rice are my top choices, but you could also use short grain white or brown rice if that's what you have in your pantry. Just be sure to use an appropriate water:rice ratio for whatever variety you choose.

2. When the rice is finished cooking, mix it with minced garlic, scallions, and lime zest while it's hot.

3. Allow it to cool slightly, and then add olive oil, sea salt, lime juice, cilantro, and jalapeño or red pepper flakes if you like your rice spicy.

4. Serve it as a side dish or use it as a component in your favorite burrito bowl!

GUEST FEATURES

Tortilla

Teddy grahams

Peanut butter

I used to make this all the time in college when I was high.

1. Spread peanut butter on 2 tortillas.

2. Top one tortilla with teddy grahams.

3. Top with the other tortilla.

4. You can heat it up in the oven but be careful because you are high (remember to turn the oven off).

TEDDY GRAHAM TORTILLA

Big Cat

- 18–24 fresh chicken wings
- 2 Tbsp baking powder
- 2 Tbsp seasoning salt
- 1 Tbsp garlic powder
- Ground black pepper
- Frank's RedHot
- ¼ cup white vinegar
- ½ stick of butter, melted
- 4 cloves of garlic, minced

This is the best way to cook wings that make you feel like you're in Buffalo but don't require cooking in batches cuz your pans are too small to fry more than 6 wings at once. They're slightly healthier than frying them, but also will impress babes more because you're using an oven, which reminds chicks of their uterus.

1. Preheat oven to 400°F. Put wings in a pot of water at a low boil for 7 minutes. This will melt away a lil fat and make them crispier. Pat them dry with a paper towel.

2. Take a ziplock bag, combine baking powder (NOT BAKING SODA), salt, garlic powder and some ground black pepper.

3. Add the dry wings to the bag and shake them up to coat them with the seasoning.

4. Put a paper thin layer of vegetable oil on a baking tray and lay the wings down on the tray. Try not to let them touch.

5. Bake for 50 minutes, turning halfway through.

6. Take Tums.

7. While wings are baking, make some sauce. Pour like half a bottle of Frank's RedHot, add white vinegar, melted butter, and minced garlic if you're feeling French.

8. Remove wings from the oven, toss them in the sauce. Eat until you puke.

BAKED CRISPY CHICKEN WINGS

PFT

158 GUEST FEATURES

HOT CHOCOLATE

KFC

1.5 packets of Swiss Miss, 2 whole packets if you ain't driving

Whole milk

Handful of small marshmallows

As a kid my parents always made us Swiss Miss hot chocolate, and they obviously followed the recipe. As an adult I realized I could break free from the shackles of my parents' ways and the manufacturer's suggested recipe. I began adding more powder to larger cups. Adding more marshmallows and more time on the microwave. Eventually I discovered the perfect blend of ingredients...with the perfect method of mixing...to create the perfect mug of hot chocolate.

1. Fill half mug (14 oz mug ideal) with whole milk.

2. Microwave for 1 minute.

3. Stir till dissolved, fill remainder of the mug.

4. Microwave for another minute (or to preferred temp).

5. Finish stirring.

6. Add more marshmallows.

NOT YOUR MOTHER'S COOKBOOK

SLEEPYTIME SANDWICH

2 Eggo waffles
Peanut butter
Ice cream of your choosing
Candy of your choosing
Maple syrup

It's three AM and you're staring at your ceiling, unable to sleep. You're either drunk, high, anxious, or sad. Probably all four. It's been almost an hour since the last time you stumbled to the kitchen in the dark and in your underwear for a snack, so it's about time for another trip but you can't decide what you want. The only cure for this insomnia is a food coma, so you have to turn to the Sleepytime Sandwich. "But will it give me a sugar high?" you wonder.

Of course not, you're not seven years old.

After navigating the cluttered bedroom floor and agilely avoiding the coffee table in the pitch black, you arrive in the kitchen. The first step is the freezer to grab Eggos, the blast of cold air feels great on your face and for a moment you feel like you're standing free in the Arctic. You pop the Eggos in the toaster. While they brown, you head back to the freezer to decide your ice cream. It's a Half Baked night, just like you. As the Eggos continue to bask in the sun, you run hot water over your scooping spoon. You're not a rookie, and you don't want the endorphins from a bicep-scoop workout to wake you up any more than you have to.

Take the Eggos out of the toaster and place them on a plate. Smear one side of both with peanut butter, this will prevent the ice cream from melting through any holes. Next, you scoop your Half Baked. With the warmed spoon it cuts like a hot knife through butter, or, alternatively, like a hot spoon through ice cream. Place the ice cream on one Eggo and top it with the other.

You could stop here if you wish, and have yourself a sandwich that's edible with your hands. But I like to press the limits. I top the sandwich with candy, M&Ms and semi-sweet chocolate chips usually, then maple syrup all over the place as a decorative piece.

You'll need a fork and knife to eat it this way, and an insulin shot for the rest of your life, but it's always worth it.

Feitelberg

NOT YOUR MOTHER'S COOKBOOK

Donnie

WONTON DON'S GOURMET 'GOONS (CRAB CLASSIC VARIETY)

8 oz pack of cream cheese

8 oz pack of imitation (or real) crab meat

2 Tbsp garlic (2 cloves)

3 Tbsp chopped green onion (approx. 2 green onions)

Half Tbsp of salt (or just salt to taste)

Sweet chili sauce (or duck sauce)

Yields approx. 20 rangoons

P.S. After mastering the Crab Classic Rangoons don't be afraid to mix it up. If you've seen my Gooned Up video series you'll know there are endless rangoon varieties. BBQ Chicken goons, Italian Beef goons, breakfast goons, dessert goons. The world is your wonton. Wrap it. Stack it. And fry that shit in oil.

Crab Rangoons aka 'GOONS are found on the menus of Chinese restaurants all over the country, but that doesn't make them Chinese food. In fact, they're as American as Apple pie. Invented in the 1950's at Trader Vic's, a Polynesian restaurant in San Francisco, 'GOONS encapsulate everything admirable about our Nation. Much like how the USA is where people from different countries come together to create their own distinct and fascinating culture, Goons are where ingredients from different cultures blend together to become something uniquely delicious. They aren't the healthiest, but neither are Americans, so break out some oil, and get GOONED UP. It's the Patriotic thing to do.

1. Dice up the garlic, green onions, and crab meat.
2. Mix in a large bowl with cream cheese.
3. Add salt to taste.
4. Place a teaspoon of the filling of each Wonton Wrapper.
5. Wet two sides of the wrapper with water or beaten egg yolk
6. Fold the wonton skin diagonally to form a triangle, pressing edges to seal. Moisten one of the bottom corners. Create a crown by pulling both bottom corners together and sealing. (Remember, there's no wrong way to wrap a wonton so don't worry if you f*ck this up. Just make sure the filling is sealed in)
7. Fry in 350°F oil until golden brown and crispy (approx. 1–3 minutes)
8. Let cool for at least 5 minutes.
9. Dip in your favorite sauce and you're officially GOONED UP!

PASTA GULAGIA

Ria

1 lb of spaghetti

2 Tbsp butter

¼ cup of olive oil

5 cloves of garlic

1 can of diced tomatoes

Pinch of salt & pepper

Pecorino Romano grated cheese

A handful of fresh basil

Pasta Gulagia is a Sicilian pasta dish that is all about the flavors. I learned how to make this from watching my Nonno make it ever since I was a little girl. It's simple and fast but gives you that authentic Italian feeling that can be eaten at any time. Most of the dishes I know how to make are Italian/Sicilian oriented because both my mom and dad are 100% Italian and they learned the recipes from their parents. When I was younger I would ask my mom to make this for me every year on my birthday and now it instantly brings a smile to my face whenever I eat it. (Which is frequently now that I know how to make it.)

Boil a pot of water, when it comes to a boil add salt then add the pasta (cook for however long the box of spaghetti you picked out says to usually 7–8 minutes but could be 10).

1. Melt 2 tablespoons of butter in a saucepan then add ¼ olive oil, crushed up garlic cloves (5 of them), can of diced tomatoes, salt & pepper.

2. Let this simmer in a pot when you put the water up for the pasta to boil and leave on simmer for as long as the pasta cooks.

3. When the spaghetti is done drain the water then add this sauce to the spaghetti, add pecorino Romano grated cheese and mix together with the sauce and spaghetti.

4. To finish, chop up some basil and add it into the mix. Now it's time to plate your dish and all you have to do is add some more pecorino Romano grated cheese to top it off.

GUEST FEATURES

1 cup of sugar

6 Tbsp flour

Pinch of salt

4 egg yolks (reserve whites for meringue)

2 cups of milk

2 tsp vanilla extract

6 Tbsp butter

4 bananas, ripe, peeled and sliced

Vanilla wafers

4 egg whites

½ cup of sugar

½ tsp of cream of tartar

Yields 8–10

There is nothing in the Walker family more cherished than my grandmother's banana pudding. I have fond memories of being locked in the basement for days at a time and subsisting on nothing but her banana pudding. One of my favorite memories is the day my dad got out of prison and all he wanted was her banana pudding and some meth. Memories.

1. Preheat the oven to 350°F.

2. Combine sugar, flour, salt, eggs, milk and vanilla in a small non-reactive saucepan. Cook over low heat, stirring constantly until the pudding thickens. Remove from heat and slowly add butter until incorporated.

3. Butter a two-quart baking dish. Arrange the vanilla wafers around the outside and across the bottom of the baking dish. Spread a layer of custard over the wafers. Place sliced bananas on top of custard and spoon the remaining custard over bananas, spreading evenly.

4. Using an electric mixer beat the egg whites until they are increased in volume. Add sugar and cream of tartar. Beat to stiff peaks. Spread meringue over pudding and bake for 8–10 minutes.

BANANA PUDDING

Brandon Walker

RON-CHILADAS

- 1 can of cream of mushroom soup
- ¼ can of cream of onion
- 1 can of cream of chicken.
- 16 ounces of sour cream.
- 2 small cans of chopped green chilies
- 2 small cans of chopped black olives
- 16 ounces of grated Mexican blend cheese
- 8 boneless chicken breasts
- 10–12 flour tortillas

These southwest-style chicken enchiladas were created by my dad, the one and only Ron Smith (hence the name Ron-chiladas). They were the #1 menu staple in our house growing up. I'm actually convinced it was my first real meal. My sister and I would ask nicely (demand) for them to be made every birthday, every special occasion and really just any time we could sweet talk my dad to get in the kitchen when he got home from work. Now when I go back to Texas (which is a rarity), it's the only thing I request. That and a good paired red wine. They're creamy. They're cheesy. They're spicy (if you want them to be). They're fucking unreal. You really just can't get enough. Basically, my dad is responsible for my two favorite things... Ron-chiladas and my love of football. Shout out to you, Dad.

1. Boil the chicken breasts in chicken bouillon (you can also grill it for additional smoky flavor).
2. Chop chicken up into bite size pieces.
3. Mix all other ingredients in a large mixing bowl.
4. Add chicken to mixing bowl and stir.
5. Add a light layer of the mix to the bottom of an oven safe dish.
6. Stuff and roll each tortilla, placing each one on top of the layer. If there is filling left, I cover the top.
7. Top with cheese.
8. Bake at 400°F for 30 minutes.
9. If desired, add salsa or hot sauce for more flavor.

Kayce Smith

BAGEL BITES

Alex Cooper

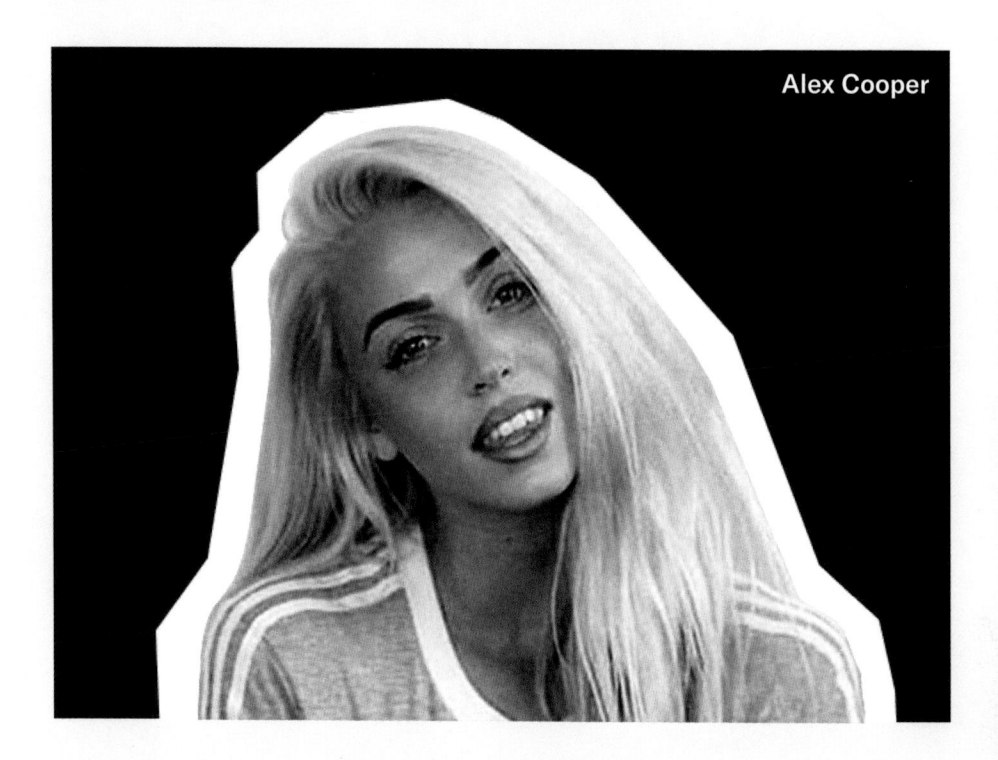

Bagel Bites

A man could beg me to let him take me to a glorious Michelin star restaurant, I could see endless delicious options on UberEats, GrubHub, Seamless, Postmates, Caviar for the night; but no matter what, my unwavering loyalty will always be to my absolute go-to, the Alex Cooper holy grail, Bagel Bites. Pop those bad boys in the oven for 15 minutes, get the edges nice and crispy, and with a nice generous side of ranch, there truly is no better satisfying meal. Cooking is not for me, but I will always go the extra mile and preheat an oven for those tasty scrumptious perfect bad boys.

MOVIE THEATER AT-HOME COMBO POPCORN

½ cup of Ghirardelli dark or semi-sweet melting chocolate (can replace with other brands)

2 Tbsp butter or margarine

1 Tbsp corn syrup

4 Tbsp unpopped popcorn

1½ Tbsp coconut oil

1 regular sized bag of M&Ms

1 square of foil, enough to cover a pot

Salt to taste

There is nothing quite like going to the movie theater and nestling in your chair with a fresh bucket of popcorn, candy, or even both! I am of the belief that every now and then popcorn mixed with chocolate, such as M&Ms or Raisenettes, is the GOAT movie snack that can take a movie viewing experience to the next level. At home? Not quite as easy as ordering the popcorn at your local theater. This recipe isn't complex, but it is fresh, salty, sweet, and a great way to elevate your at-home movie experience. This popcorn is salty, crispy, airy, and fresh, not that garbage in the bag you get at a grocery store. Then when you toss on some chocolate and throw in some M&Ms? It simply can't be beat!

Popcorn:

1. Put the coconut oil in a pot over medium heat, with two kernels.
2. Place tin foil over the pot, puncturing holes in the top.
3. When you hear the first kernel pop, empty in the remaining kernels.
4. Shake repeatedly until the popcorn begins to slow down to a near stop.
5. Immediately put popped popcorn into a bowl, salt to taste.
6. Optional: Melt butter, if needed, but it will be fine as it is.

Chocolate drizzle:

1. Place melting chocolate, butter/margarine, corn syrup into a microwavable bowl.
2. Microwave the contents for 1.5 to 2 minutes, or until smooth enough to stir.
3. Remove bowl from microwave and stir until silky smooth.

Jeff Lowe

NOT YOUR MOTHER'S COOKBOOK

SECOND GREATEST CHOCOLATE CHIP COOKIE IN THE WORLD

Everyone loves chocolate chip cookies, but let's be real, they are NOT all created equally. Don't get me wrong, if you put a freshly baked cookie in front of me, I will eat it, but there's something special about a classic, simple cookie done extraordinarily well. In my opinion that means Levain Bakery. Their chocolate chip cookie is, without question, the best chocolate chip cookie I have ever had. Period.

Naturally, when the quarantine rolled into town, I made it my mission to duplicate the legend.

Spoiler alert: I failed.

After many, many batches and alterations, I eventually gave up; it just couldn't be done. Sure, I could bake a cookie that was pretty damn close to the OG, but it still wasn't the real thing and that comparison depreciated what would otherwise be a solid cookie. So I decided to abandon the original mission and instead create the Second Greatest Chocolate Chip Cookie in the World.

If you can't beat 'em, get right behind 'em.

Liz Gonzales

GUEST FEATURES

½ cup of unsalted butter, melted (be sure you let it cool for 7–8 minutes before you use it otherwise it may melt the sugar, leaving you with a runny mess)

¾ cup of light brown sugar (make sure you pack this bad boy)

¼ cup of sugar

1 egg at room temp

½ tsp vanilla extract

1–1½ Tbsp maple syrup (I know this may sound weird, but it's crucial. Trust the process. And no the cookies will not taste like pancakes.)

1½ cups + 2 Tbsp of all-purpose flour (3¼ cups if you're doubling the recipe)

1 tsp cornstarch

½ tsp baking powder

½ tsp baking soda

½ tsp salt

1 cup of semisweet chips

½ cup of dark chocolate chips or chunks (you can use all semisweet but I think the dark chocolate adds a certain je ne sais quoi)

¾ cup of walnuts (I need a nut in my cookie, but if that's not your jam, just leave them out)

Note: I live alone so this recipe only produces about 8 pretty hefty cookies. Double up if you live with someone other than a pup because, trust me, they'll want in on the action. I usually bake 3 or 4 cookies at a time and put the remaining dough in the fridge so I can enjoy freshly baked cookies the next day. You can also freeze the dough and stick it in the fridge to defrost for a couple of hours before you're ready to use it if you plan on waiting longer than a couple of days between bakes.

Bowl 1:

1. Whisk together the melted, cooled butter and both sugars.

2. Whisk in the egg.

3. Add the vanilla extract and maple syrup.

Bowl 2:

4. Whisk together dry ingredients: flour, cornstarch, baking powder, baking soda, and salt.

Combine:

5. In bowl one, add in bowl two slowly until everything is perfectly combined.

6. Stir in chocolate chips and walnuts.

7. VERY IMPORTANT STEP: cover the dough with plastic wrap and put that shiz in the fridge for at least 45 minutes. Bare minimum. I know the waiting sucks, but it's what gets the consistency juuuust right.

8. Preheat your oven to 350°F while you're anxiously waiting and place parchment paper on your cookie sheets to get them ready to go come game time. And no, you don't have to use parchment paper, but I find they bake better with the paper and it minimizes clean up.

9. Post chilling, scoop big balls of the dough (around 2–3 tablespoons) and make sure they're a little taller than they are wide for a better bake.

10. Place on a cookie sheet and bake for 10–14 minutes. Every oven is slightly different so keep an eye on them. They will look a little raw in the middle, but once the edges start to get that golden crisp, take them out as they will continue to cook a bit on the cookie sheet.

11. Let them cool down on the cookie sheet. Do not transfer them to a wire rack before they're cool—they need the sheet love.

12. Tear 'em up!

NOT YOUR MOTHER'S COOKBOOK

STUFFED MUSHROOMS

People don't like to talk about it, but the Mick Man is Italian. That's right. I'm as surprised as you are seeing as I'm the whitest person alive. But it's true. My father was Italian, and while he wasn't in the kitchen every night, when he did stand over the stove we knew we were in for good eating. The holidays especially brought out his desire to flex, and the one thing that consistently brought the house down was stuffed mushrooms.

Merely an appetizer but would leave the crowd more than ready to spoil its entire appetite before the main course began. His recipe was simple: breadcrumbs and butter. But what kind of man would I be if I simply copy and pasted his recipe and didn't add to it for the next generation? I decided to take it up several more notches.

Coley Mick

2 packs of large white mushrooms

Olive oil

Marsala wine

1 lb of ground sweet sausage

Garlic, minced

1 cup of breadcrumbs

6 oz mascarpone

Grated parmesan

1 large bowl

1 large pan

2 baking sheets

1. Set the oven to 325°F.

2. Pop out the stems from the mushrooms. There are a few methods to do this correctly so you don't fuck up the mushroom caps' integrity. Some people prefer the twist, others prefer the dig. Whatever floats your boat. Put the caps into the large bowl with some olive oil and Marsala and toss 'em together. Get your hands in there, really massage these suckers nicely.

3. Save some of the stems and finely chop them.

4. Fire up the stovetop. Add olive oil to your pan. Remember, we're cooking this Italian style here so don't rely too heavily on exact measurements. Add the sausage to the pan and break it up like you would any ground meat you were trying to brown. Cook until brown.

5. Add the chopped mushroom stems to the party for a couple of minutes. Let them get acquainted with one another. Constantly be stirring every time you're adding something. I shouldn't have to tell you this but I've seen how some of you cook, you need the help.

6. Now do the same with the garlic. A couple minced cloves will do you swell here, don't go crazy.

7. Breadcrumb time. You want a little less than a full cup. Or use a full cup, I'm not gonna tell anybody. It's a free country. Spread it around, get it all mixed together.

8. Grab your mascarpone. These typically come in 8 oz containers. You don't want to use all 8, but half isn't quite enough. I'd suggest scooping out half, mixing that in, and then adding in another couple of scoops until what you have cooking in the pan looks nice and creamy consistent throughout.

9. Finally sprinkle some parmesan all over the place. This isn't the star of the show here it's just a role player, keep that in mind.

10. Grab a teaspoon and start stuffing your mushroom caps with your mixture. Fill as desired but they should certainly be overflowing. Otherwise, what was the point?

11. Place the mushrooms on your baking sheets and toss them into the oven for about 45 minutes. If your oven sucks it might take a little longer, but 45 should be enough.

12. There will certainly be some stuffing leftover, eat that with a spoon while the mushrooms are in the oven. That's just a little secret between you and me.

13. Enjoy. You're welcome.

BROWNIES

I got into baking one night after watching the *Great British Bake Off* as I was falling asleep. I watched the show because of how calm it felt; the plain instructions, the delicious products of a little hard work. It was straightforward.

That Sunday night as I fell asleep, I told myself "I'm going to bake this week." But I didn't stop there. I told myself "I'm going to bake five cakes this week. One for each day of the week." On *The Great British Bake Off* they whip up a couple dishes an episode, so how hard could it be.

The next night I gathered my supplies and baking instruments, only to find out I was woefully short on some essential tools. Steeped in my resolve, I trudged forward, as my muscles grew sore from mixing sticks of butter into batter. There are machines for that, it seems.

Some five hours later, I had a slightly dilapidated, slightly soap-tasting cake. To an outsider it probably looked disgusting, but because it was mine, it looked beautiful. It was more satisfying than it was delicious. In a world where it sometimes feels like we have to figure out everything for ourselves, the straightforward steps and tangible product made baking a perfect calming evening hobby.

This recipe won't take you five hours and it's way harder to get wrong. Simple, delicious, gooey brownies. Start something and finish it, all in one night. You'll feel satisfied and I'm sure everyone that gets to share the brownies won't mind either.

Rone

1 stick of butter, melted
1 Tbsp cooking oil
1⅛ Tbsp regular old sugar
2 eggs
2 tsp pure vanilla extract
½ cup of flour
½ cup of unsweetened cocoa powder
¼ tsp salt

1. Preheat the oven to 350°F.

2. Find your cooking pan. It could be 9 by 9. It could be a 8 by 6.5 disposable baking pan. Obviously the size of the pan will affect the thickness of the brownies, which will play into the length of cooking time. Bigger pan = shorter cooking time.

3. Trace the bottom of the pan on a sheet of wax paper. Cut out the outline of the wax paper, and use oil or butter on the pan and on the paper. This will keep your brownies from sticking.

4. Melt the stick of butter in a bowl in the microwave.

5. Combine melted butter, oil and sugar together in a medium-sized bowl. Whisk the shit out of it til your forearm is sore.

6. Add the eggs and vanilla; beat it for another full minute.

7. Sift in flour, salt and cocoa. Just fold over the mix until the power has taken to the mix. It might feel like you didn't mix it enough, but you want to do it just the most gentle amount, and too much beatin' will ruin your batch. Too much will make the brownies cake up and will take away from that fudgy taste you want.

8. Pour the mixture into the pan you've selected on top of the wax paper.

9. Put the mix on the top shelf.

10. Bake. The length of baking will depend on your size of pan and the strength of your oven, but this could take as little as 18 minutes or as many as 25. I would definitely As soon as I start to smell brownie in the air, I know it's time to pull them, because I want these MFers to be fudgy and they will cook a little extra in the pan.

11. To see if they're ready, use a fork or toothpick. The top/center should seem congealed and the toothpick should come out with some nice residue.

12. Let those bad boys sit 'til you can't wait any longer, then serve 'em up.

NOT YOUR MOTHER'S COOKBOOK 175

PUTTANESCA SAUCE

2 Tbsp extra virgin olive oil

4 cloves garlic, thinly sliced

8 anchovy fillets packed in oil

2 Tbsp tomato paste

1 28 oz can whole peeled tomatoes, drained

Kosher salt

Freshly ground black pepper

½ cup pitted kalamata olives

¼ cup drained capers

½ tsp crushed red pepper flakes

1 Tbsp chopped fresh basil

Zest of 1 lemon

Its name translates roughly from Italian to "sauce of the whores." The origin of the dish dates back to World War II, where a large percentage of women in wartime Italy resorted to prostitution as their only viable career choice. And since the dish's pungent mix of anchovies, olives, and capers had some similarities to the scent of a mid-century Italian prostitute (allegedly), the "sauce of the whores" was born.

This sauce is very briny, so, if you're a fan of pickles, capers, and other vinegar based ingredients, you'll probably love Puttanesca... However, if you're not a fan of salty-acidic flavors, I wouldn't attempt this one. Plus... With the help of a little red wine... It goes down easier than a wartime prostitute. Enjoy.

1. Warm oil in a large pot over medium heat. Add garlic and anchovies; cook until garlic is lightly golden and anchovies melt into the oil, 3-4 minutes.

2. Add tomato paste and cook, stirring, for 2 minutes.

3. Add tomatoes and crush them with a wooden spoon. Season to taste with salt & pepper.

4. Raise heat to medium-high and cook, stirring occasionally, until tomatoes break down and mixture becomes saucy, about 10 minutes.

5. Stir in olives, capers, basil, and red pepper flakes, reduce heat to low, and simmer, stirring occasionally, until it thickens, about 30 minutes.

6. Remove from heat and stir in lemon zest.

7. Take a report.

Large

COD FISH BALLS

Willie Colon

3 bags of cod fish

1½ green pepper, chopped

1½ large onion, chopped

5 eggs

Goya red hot pickled peppers, chopped

Aunt Jemima flour

Paprika

Garlic powder

Thyme leaves

Black pepper

Goya Adobo (Light)

Water

We looked forward to my mom's Bacalaitos. They were always cooked for family gatherings so when she made them we knew we were going to have a good time. We knew they were filled with love.

1. Soak cod fish before cooking, changing the water 2 to 3 times.

2. Cook the cod fish for about an hour and half in simmering water until tender.

3. Drain water off and chop fish

4. In a large bowl mix together cod fish, green peppers, onions, eggs, hot red pepper, and all the seasonings. Then add the flour slowly until the mixture becomes crumbly. Then add water and mix until the batter becomes gooey/sticky. If the batter becomes too loose add more flour.

5. Heat a pot of vegetable oil over medium heat for 10 minutes.

6. When the oil is hot ready drop the batter in oil using a tablespoon or small scoop.

HOAGIE DIP

½ lb Genoa salami

½ lb hot Capicola ham

½ lb imported ham (like Italian roasted/boiled ham)

½ lb mild provolone cheese

½ lb white American cheese (not yellow!!! for the love of God)

2 tsp dried oregano

2 tsp dried basil

2 tsp garlic powder

Little bit of salt & pepper

6 Tbsp mayonnaise (real mayo, not the fake stuff!)

2 Tbsp red wine vinegar

1 Tbsp extra virgin olive oil

2 small onions, minced

2 chopped tomatoes

1 head of shredded lettuce, and shred it up really well

Tip: Go the grocery store during non-peak hours bc you're about to hold up the deli folks for a second.

Communions, wakes, pool parties, baby/bridal showers... If you live in the Philadelphia area and have a reliable Aunt there's one thing you can count on at any of these events: A killer Hoagie Dip.

At our family reunion week down the Jersey Shore each year I sniff it out like a shark to chum and can be found post-bars in a relative's fridge at 3am eating this stuff with my bare hands. All the best flavors of a top notch Italian hoagie chopped up for perfect bites. Yes, it's a bit pricey with all the deli meats, but my God is it worth it.

1. Stack up the deli meats and cheeses & slice/chop 'em into little pieces. You want everything to be in ¼ to ½ inch bits.

2. Stir it all together.

3. Toss in the seasonings & mayo, then the red wine vinegar. Mix it up!

4. Keep cold until it's time to serve & then toss in the chopped tomato and lettuce. If you're feeling wild toss some finely chopped hot peppers in there, too.

5. To serve it, have little pieces of bread (like you'd have for bruschetta) all sliced up & drizzled in olive oil next to the hoagie dip bowl. You can always add more mayo, etc. and salt to taste, etc. I have eaten this shit straight up with spoons & with my bare hands after nights at the bar—it's expensive to make with all the deli meats & such but it's incredible.

Shout out to my Aunt Rita who makes it better than anyone else.

Kate

NOT YOUR MOTHER'S COOKBOOK 179

SMOKED TRI-TIP

3 lbs tri-tip

1 part freshly ground coarse black pepper

1 part sea salt

¼ part garlic powder

Hickory/white oak

2 Tbsp butter

Thyme

Rosemary

Asparagus

I'm a huge fan of tri-tip. It's tender and super easy to cook.

I usually buy one on the bigger side of things at around 3lbs.

About an hour or 90 minutes before I cook it, I'll take it out of the fridge and season it.

For me, it's easy. I cook beef in a traditional Texas style and let the meat speak. I will dust both sides with equal parts freshly ground coarse black pepper and sea salt with about ¼ of the amount of garlic powder.

After it's seasoned like a sexy little bitch, I'll let it sit in the microwave (so my cat Sprinkle Dinkles doesn't touch it).

While it's resting and coming to room temp, I'll start my Big Green Egg. I set it to 225°F and have one chunk of either hickory or white oak on top of the coals.

When the tri-tip is ready and I'm about 90 minutes to 2 hours away from dinner, I toss the meat on my smoker with that fat cap on top. The fat will render and keep everything all juicy.

When the internal temp of the meat reaches 125, I pull it from the low heat and set it aside while I raise the temp of the Big Green Egg to 550–600. I'll have a cast iron skillet on hand and that warms while the grill does.

When it's 550, I'll open the Egg and toss in 2 tablespoons of butter, a few sprigs of thyme, and a touch of rosemary. When that melts and the butter begins turning brown, I'll sear the non-fat cap side of the meat. It takes about 2 minutes.

After I remove the meat again, I'll toss on the asparagus at the same 550, close the Egg, and walk into my house with the meat tray. I'll say to my beloved bride, "looks great, right honey?" She will dismissively say yes and I'll smile.

After setting the meat down and loosely covering it, I'll hurry back outside and get the asparagus off. It takes about 3–4 minutes at that heat.

When the meat has rested 10–15 minutes, cut it, serve it with the asparagus, ask everyone how they like it a few times, and give the remaining pieces to your dog named Gus.

When that's all done, tell your older kid to clean up the kitchen and go close the vents on your Big Green Egg.

Chaps

NOT YOUR MOTHER'S COOKBOOK 181

3 lbs of sweet onions

4 Tbsp of butter

½ cup of wine

Garlic

Beef stock

Worcestershire sauce

Thyme

Bay leaf

Salt and pepper

Bread

Cheese

I think French Onion Soup is the ultimate starter before you have a nice steak dinner. In fact any good steak place that has it instantly bumps up a point in my eyes. From the flavor to the cheese to the beautiful crock it's served in it all in all makes it an elite soup.

1. Cut 2–3 lbs of sweet onions into rings or half rings.

2. Put large pot on medium heat with melted butter or olive oil (or both) and salt/pepper to taste.

3. Put onions in and stir every 5 minutes to keep them from burning, trying to caramelize, will take 30–40 minutes.

4. Once cooked to preference, add half a cup wine (any cooking wine) to deglaze.

5. Add beef stock (I prefer low-sodium stock and add my own salt), thyme—super important seasoning, garlic (can use powder if needed), bay leaf, Worcestershire sauce, salt/pepper to taste, simmer for 30–60 minutes low heat.

6. Have your bread/cheese preference ready.

7. Pour soup into bowls, put bread (sliced baguette is best, but really whatever the largest piece of bread that fits in there) and cheese (whichever you prefer provolone, gruyere, etc.) in oven and broil for 2 minutes top...Don't be shy with the cheese as it should cover the whole bowl like a pool cover. No half-assing.

FRENCH ONION SOUP

Eddie

GUEST FEATURES

CHICKEN CACCIATORE

Frankie

1 roasted chicken, broken down into 8 pieces

1 onion sliced

1 red pepper

1 green pepper

2 cups fresh mushroom

2 cloves of garlic

Pinch of salt & pepper

2 Tbsp butter

4 Tbsp olive oil

1 can of whole or diced tomatoes

½ cup of white wine

Chopped parsley

Pinch of oregano

Red pepper flakes (optional)

Parmigiana cheese (for sprinkling)

This Chicken Cacciatore recipe dates back to 1955 when my Grandfather put together the first Borrelli's menu. Back then, this dish cost just $1.80. The cacciatore, on the bone specifically, is one of my personal favorites and has always been my go to recommendation for new customers at the restaurant.

1. Cook chicken in a 350°F oven until fully cooked, then cut into 8 pieces.
2. Place a pan on medium heat and add butter and olive oil.
3. Add the sliced onions and peppers and saute until brown.
4. Add the garlic and mushrooms.
5. Add the white wine.
6. Add the can of tomatoes and pinch of oregano.
7. Add chicken pieces to pan.
8. Cover and simmer for 15–20 minutes until the chicken is tender.
9. Sprinkle with cheese and fresh parsley to serve.

NOT YOUR MOTHER'S COOKBOOK

POTATO SOUP

Brianna Chickenfry

6 slices bacon

6 medium size potatoes

1 small yellow onion

1 cup heavy whipping cream

1 cup cheddar cheese, plus more for garnish

4 Tbsp butter

2 Tbsp flour

Chicken broth

Garlic powder

Pepper

Salt

1. Cut bacon into small squares and put them on a baking sheet and cook in oven until crispy.

2. Dice onion.

3. Sauté the onion in a large soup pot until soft.

4. Then add bacon and grease to the onions.

5. Cut potatoes into cubes. Put them in a pan with onion and bacon. Steam for 2 minutes.

6. Pour chicken broth into a pot until potatoes are covered.

7. Cook until potatoes are soft on medium heat.

8. In a separate pan, melt butter.

9. Once butter is melted, add flour.

10. Once that is thick like dough, add heavy whipping cream in and mix until dough is mixed well into cream. Then add the cheddar cheese to the mixture.

11. Add that roux to the potatoes and broth and then cook until well blended, 10 minutes on high heat.

12. Top with cheese, salt, pepper, garlic powder!

3 cheeses (2 hard, 1 soft)

3 meats

Crackers or sliced baguette (I prefer baguette)

That's all you need for a great board! Can you add to that? Sure, but if you have to ask, "does this belong?" then it probably doesn't. Also, if it requires a fork or can't be eaten with your hand, leave it off.

The thing to remember about a charcuterie board is it's hard to be wrong but it's also easy to be not right. If I've learned anything in the charc game is that sometimes people try to do too much. I've also learned that people get very defensive of their boards. Stick with this recipe and you can't go wrong.

For me I would start with:

- Brie
- Smoked Gouda
- Parmigiano Reggiano
- Prosciutto
- Saucisson
- Sopressata

If you don't like one of those, sub it out for a meat that you like! Sometimes if I can get duck or venison involved, I'll jump at the chance. Nuts, olives, jams, mini pickles, are all ways to dress up your board. The wildest thing I like on my board are chocolate covered pretzels—unconventional but the salty/sweet combo works for me.

Finally, PRESENTATION is key! Slice your meat and cheese cleanly. Plate it in an organized fashion. Meat and cheese that invites you to party always tastes better. Oh, and a little vino alongside your board never hurt nobody.

CONS CHARCUTERIE

Captain Cons

IDIOT'S CHICKEN

Chicken cutlets sliced thin

Egg

Bread crumbs

Italian dressing

Tomato

White rice

This was passed down from one idiot to another (me) and it's a go-to meal, for a date, or living alone. Super easy and tasteful.

So easy an idiot can make it.

1. Cut up tomatoes into small pieces and cook them in low low heat in Italian dressing.

2. Fry up a chicken cutlet, put the mix over the chicken and white rice.

Yours in picks,

Rico Bo$co

"Some things are bigger than sports."

NOT YOUR MOTHER'S COOKBOOK   187

CLOSING

Welcome to the end of the cookbook! I hope you have found it useful. If you are brand new to cooking and this is the first time you have really given it a go, I hope I have helped take some stress away from the process. It may still be difficult for you, but please do not get discouraged. Like any new skill in life, cooking takes time and practice to develop. Use this book as a reference, keep practicing, and keep cooking. You'll be amazed at how fast the learning curve is. Get in that kitchen and make a fucking mess—take the basic principles I have taught you in this book and create new dishes of your own. You'll notice that after you learn the basics, cooking will go from a chore to an outlet for creative expression, and that's when it gets really fun.

I'd like to thank everyone who was involved in making this book come to life. Especially Dave Portnoy and Erika Nardini, without them none of this would be possible. I'd also like to thank my uncle, Chris Johnson, for inspiring me to begin cooking in the first place. As well as my parents, Lisa and Al, for allowing me to chase my dreams.

GLOSSARY

<u>Bake/Roast</u>: To cook using dry heat. This is done in an oven or countertop convection oven. This may be getting slightly technical but the difference between roasting and baking comes down to two major factors; food structure and oven temperature. We associate baking with foods that lack a solid structure before entering the oven (think doughs, cake batters, cookies, etc.). Baking is done at a lower temperature—typically not higher than 375°F—whereas roasting always occurs above 400°F and is associated with food that has a solid structure prior to entering the oven (think meat and vegetables).

<u>Baste</u>: To apply a liquid or sauce to your food during the cooking process. Basting can be done with drippings from the pan to double down on flavor. Often, you baste a protein with melted butter right before it is served. Basting helps keep food nice and moist while increasing the depth of flavor.

<u>Braise</u>: To cook food partially covered in liquid on a low simmer. Braising is how you turn those cheap cuts of meats into melt-in-your-mouth flavor-packed bites. This is where searing comes into play, a good sear on your protein is crucial to a successful braise. The braising liquid is also often used to build a beautiful finishing sauce simply by reducing it down once the cooking is completed.

<u>Bread</u>: To bread something is to coat first with flour, then place in beaten eggs or milk, and finish by placing in crushed stale breadcrumbs, cereal, or your favorite cracker to create, you guessed it, a breading. You take this breaded protein and either pan fry, deep fry, or bake it to create a crispy coating on our food.

<u>Broil</u>: To cook using direct heat. Ovens have a 'broiler' which is an exposed coil pumping constant heat directly onto what you are cooking. Broiling is often done, but not limited, to finishing a dish when you need to create a quick crust or char on your food, melt cheese or crisp up poultry skin.

<u>Caramelize</u>: To cook sugar on a low heat until it turns golden brown. We say 'caramelized' onions because they are full of natural sugars, which we slowly turn into a sticky caramel.

<u>Chop/Rough chop</u>: To roughly cut an ingredient into pieces that are relatively the same size. When a recipe called for a chop or rough chop you do not need to worry about how precise the ingredient is cut up, simply chop it into around half-inch cubes.

<u>Dice</u>: Nearly the same as chopping only when you dice

you want to try to keep everything the same size. For the purposes of this book when I use the term dice that will mean to cut into ¼-inch cubes.

Dredge: To place food in flour or a spice mix until it is covered. You see this come up in the breading process.

Deglaze: To pour liquid over a hot pan full of fond from searing or roasting. The deglazing process helps gather all the remaining flavor in a pan. The fond is scraped and reduced with the deglazing liquid to form a quick pan sauce.

Fillet: A piece of meat, fish, or poultry with all bones taken out. To fillet something is to take out all the bones.

Fond: The brown bits left in a pan after searing or roasting protein. The fond is full of flavor and should always be deglazed to form a quick pan sauce. If you leave the fond, all the flavor is going right into your sink.

Marinate: To let food sit in seasonings that typically includes at least one wet ingredient, and an acid; such as wine, vinegar, or strong citrus fruits, to tenderize and increase the flavor. This process can be anywhere from 30 minutes to 24 hours. I have found marinades to be most effective at the 12-hour mark. If you marinate for too little time, you will not reap the benefits of infused flavor and tenderized meat. However if you marinade for too long, you can over-tenderize your meat and be left with a mushy, unsavory texture.

Mince: To cut food into very small pieces. Think dicing but trying to get the ingredient as small as possible. Mincing is most effective when you place your free hand on top of the blade of your knife and rock it back and forth across the ingredient you are mincing.

Pan fry: Much like sautéing, when we pan fry we are cooking whole proteins to completion in just one pan on the stovetop. The difference with pan frying is we are using more oil. The oil is what is cooking our food rather than the direct heat from the pan.

Poach: To cook slowly in a liquid that is just below boiling. You can poach in water, broth or milk. Eggs are what you typically associate with poaching but you can make delicious fish by poaching.

Purée: To put food through a blender or food processor in order to produce a thick pulp.

Reduce: To boil down a liquid to concentrate the flavor. Reducing is very common when making sauces.

Render: To melt fat away very slowly at a low temperature. If you want perfectly crispy bacon bits you must slowly render away the fat.

Sauté: To cook an ingredient quickly in a pan with a little bit of butter or oil on high heat. The goal here is to get the ingredient browned and build flavor in the dish. Searing is a form of sautéing.

Sear: Searing is an essential step to cooking protein. Searing builds a crust on your meat which creates a seal, locking in all the juices. You can cook a protein to completion quickly by searing it, or we can use searing to brown cheap cuts of protein that we will later braise and cook slowly. Whether it be for a beautiful ribeye steak or a cheap cut of stewing beef, the sear is crucial to the flavor of a dish. To properly sear you need your pan on high heat. Open your windows, and turn on the fan. Get ready to hear a sizzle and see some smoke. You only get one shot at creating a sear on a piece of meat so be patient. If you go to turn your protein and it isn't pulling away with ease, wait. Don't force a flip, the crust hasn't formed yet, wait till the protein comes off cleanly.

Score: To make small slits in food, usually only a few centimeters in depth. This is done to create texture when cooking, increase flavor penetration of a marinade, and to prevent skin or a fat cap from curling.

Simmer: To cook a sauce just below the boiling point. This is done to concentrate flavors and allow a sauce to build in depth.

Steam: To cook in a mesh/perforated container over boiling water. This is commonly used for cooking vegetables, fish, and dumplings.

Stir fry: To cook in a frying pan over high heat. This is done very quickly and the contents of the pan must be continuously stirred to prevent it from burning.

Sweat: To cook vegetables gently on a low heat with oil or butter in a covered pan or pot. This is similar to sautéing only in this method you are not looking for any browning. When you sweat you are looking for a more mild release of flavor, when you sauté you create a stronger flavor and add sweetness. Sweating is done typically as a base for sauces and soups.

Zest: To grate the outer layer of a citrus fruit. Zesting adds strong flavor and a little goes a long way. Make sure when zesting not to get any of the pith (the white part) of the fruit, it is very bitter and can ruin the flavor of a dish.

Acknowledgements

Designer Kelly Na

Photographer Bryan Gardner

Food Stylist Pearl Jones

Proofreaders Alex Rosenthal, Allison Saul, Eric Nathan, Jack Wolfe, Peter Frommelt, Pilar Pitalue

© 2020 Barstool Sports, Inc.

All rights reserved. Neither this book, nor any part thereof, may be reproduced in any form without the express written permission of Barstool Sports, Inc.

All trademarks referenced or depicted herein are the property of their respective owners. No reference to any third party product or brand in this book should be seen as an endorsement thereof.